PORTFOLIO
BUSINESS AND INTELLECTUAL PROPERTY

Anurag K. Agarwal is a mechanical engineer from MNREC, Allahabad (now known as MNNIT). After working for less than a year with Bharat Petroleum, he decided to study law. He completed his LL.B., LL.M., and LL.D. from Lucknow University and second LL.M. from Harvard Law School. He practised as an Advocate at Lucknow for about seven years and for about a year and a half at Delhi, then switched over to full-time teaching in 2004, with a brief stint at MDI Gurgaon. He has been with IIMA since then in the Business Policy Area and has been the Chairperson of the Post Graduate Programme in Public Management and Policy (PGPPMP) at IIMA. He is also a visiting faculty at ESSEC, Paris. His teaching and research interests include intellectual property, dispute resolution, and relationship between business, government, and law.

INDIA'S BESTSELLING BUSINESS BOOKS SERIES

AHMEDABAD
BUSINESS BOOKS

BUSINESS AND INTELLECTUAL PROPERTY

Protect Your Idea

ANURAG K. AGARWAL

PORTFOLIO
PENGUIN

An imprint of Penguin Random House

PORTFOLIO

USA | Canada | UK | Ireland | Australia
New Zealand | India | South Africa | China | Singapore

Portfolio is part of the Penguin Random House group of companies
whose addresses can be found at global.penguinrandomhouse.com

Published by Penguin Random House India Pvt. Ltd
4th Floor, Capital Tower 1, MG Road,
Gurugram 122 002, Haryana, India

Penguin
Random House
India

First published in Random Business by Random House India 2010
Published by Penguin Random House India 2016
Published in Portfolio by Penguin Random House India 2018

ISBN 9788184001402

Printed at Repro India Limited

www.penguin.co.in

This is a legitimate digitally printed version of the book and therefore might not
have certain extra finishing on the cover.

To my parents,

Smt Bimla Devi Agarwal
and
Shri Ram Lakhan Agarwal, Advocate

CONTENTS

Preface

The book is a part of the IIM Ahmedabad—Random House Business Book Series and deals with intellectual property from a business perspective. The book is not meant for experts in intellectual property rights. It is also not a textbook on intellectual property rights, but meant for readers without any background in the area. It is assumed, however, that they do have a keen sense of business in general. A reading of the book shall make them curious to know more about different branches of IP and how they can relate their business to commercial exploitation of intellectual property. As the global effort is to protect intellectual property and also to harmonize laws in different jurisdictions, it is now imperative for astute business managers to understand the basic concepts of different branches of IP and put forth their best efforts for the protection of their intellectual property. The book provides just a window to such opportunities and possibilities.

The book starts with an introductory chapter, a hypothetical situation called 'The Pomegranate Story' and describes the relationship between business and intellectual property, and how companies may use IP rights to advance their interests. The story tells us about different types of intellectual property—patents, copyrights, trademarks, designs, geographical indications, and trade secrets. Each shall be discussed in separate chapters with the help of landmark cases primarily from Indian and American courts. These court judgments are in the public domain and can be used by anyone. In fact, the effort should be wider dissemination of these judgments, as these are an integral part of the 'law of the land'. I have not always given the entire judgment—only the important parts have been culled. I have made an effort to devoid them of legal jargon so that they are palatable to everyone. In this process, I have tried to retain the original feel and flavour of the judgments. Selection of the cases has been made in a manner to highlight the topic concerned and in relation to the name of a product or company with which the reader would be familiar. To enhance readability, I have selectively omitted citations and footnotes.

There are other types of intellectual property also recognized by the TRIPS—layout design of semi-conductors, plant varieties and farmers' rights, anti-competitive practices in contractual licences, etc., which have not been discussed in the book.

My sincere thanks to Professor Samir K. Barua, Director, IIMA for conceptualizing the Business Book series. Special thanks to RHI and its entire team, particularly to Chiki and Priyanka, who made this possible. Thanks to Ms Denise E. Gardener who provided research assistance and Mrs Ramany Vijayapalan for providing secretarial assistance. Thanks to my sons—Anant and Akshat—who allowed me to work at all odd hours, even on holidays and weekends; and my wife—Manjari—for everything.

October 8, 2010

1

Introduction

Intellectual property, as the name suggests, is the creation of intellect. It is primarily a thought, an idea, a plan, a scheme, a method to make something new—but something that also includes further steps to make it possible, to make it work. It should not just remain an idea. As ideas can be shared without the original owner being deprived of the idea, it becomes extremely difficult to detect theft. Protection needs to be provided to such thinkers to come up with new ideas. Evolved jurisdictions have enacted laws to protect intellectual property so as to encourage inventors, poets, artists, businesses, etc. Intellectual property laws typically give the owner of any intellectual property the exclusive right to use it. Others are barred from using it without the consent of the owner. This right, given by law, puts the owner in an enviable position, but a balance needs to be achieved so that society benefits in equal measure.

The global arrangement by TRIPS (Agreement related to Trade Related Intellectual Property Rights) under the auspices of the World Trade Organization (WTO), is a step in that direction. With geographical boundaries losing relevance in the field of information sharing, handling intellectual property issues in a holistic manner for the world is the need of the hour. Efforts in the field of intellectual property to harmonize the law and other practices have been undertaken for more than a century, however, there has been tremendous momentum in the last decade and a half.

Let us start with a story which tells us about the importance of intellectual property and its different branches.

THE POMEGRANATE STORY

Himanshu, a graduate from one of the leading engineering colleges in India went on to do his postgraduate diploma in management from one of the leading management schools in India. He was employed with one of the most prestigious consultancy firms in New York and worked there for more than five years. He was quite satisfied and happy with his work as he used to be presented with new challenges in his professional life and because of his good education coupled with amiable personality and positive attitude, he was able to take all the challenges in stride.

The Will

One evening, when he had returned from the office, he received a letter from a lawyer in India. To his utter surprise, the letter mentioned that one of his uncles, who used to live in Anarabad in India, had passed away and in his will bequeathed all his property — which included about 1000 acres of pomegranate orchards— to Himanshu. He had mixed feelings as he fondly remembered spending some time in his childhood on the orchards and adjoining farms with his uncle. He did not know what to do, so he called his mother who was leading a holy, sacred, spiritual, and healthy lifestyle at an Ashram in Haridwar, in the foothills of the Himalayas. His mother told him that it was for him to make up his mind whether to continue living in New York or get a taste of the simple life at Anarabad.

Since his childhood, Himanshu always had a fascination for life on a farm—in the midst of nature, greenery, trees, animals, etc. He also thought that he could come back to his job or a similar job anytime, so he made up his mind to give life at Anarabad a try.

Anarabad

Anarabad is a small town situated at NH-8. The place has always been famous for its pomegranates—juicy and delicious—and had recently been registered with the Geographical Indication in India. The pomegranates from Anarabad are so famous that any person passing through the town—whether by bus or car—will surely stop to buy fresh pomegranates which are always available at throwaway prices. It also has a railway station where hawkers sell freshly picked pomegranates. The place is well-known for the best quality pomegranates and local life revolves around the fruit. Even the names of local persons reflect the connection with the pomegranate or Anar in Hindi. It is not uncommon to find men named Anarlal, Anarchand, Anarbhai, Anarsingh, Anardas, etc. A number of women were named Anaramati, Anaradevi, Anarakumari, and the most popular being Anarkali. If a person visits any house in Anarabad, the first thing to be offered is fresh pomegranate juice, followed by a bowl of pomegranate seeds. Almost every recipe in Anarabad includes Anardana—the pomegranate seeds. Pomegranate picking tours and contests are organized regularly. Buses loaded with school children often reach Anarabad from nearby places to enjoy a picnic at one of the pomegranate orchards. Different uses of pomegranate seeds, skin, juice, etc., are known to the local people and have become a part of traditional knowledge in Anarabad.

The Problem of Plenty

Himanshu reached Anarabad and his uncle's estate manager reported to him and told him that they have about 1000 acres of pomegranate orchards. In the evening the manager came with dozens of baskets full of pomegranates and asked him what to do with them. He didn't have a clue and requested the manager to do what he has been doing for so many years. The manager informed him that he would go and sell the pomegranates in the local wholesale fruit market. The next morning the manager came back with a couple of thousand rupees and told Himanshu that this was what he got for all the pomegranates. Himanshu was shocked. Still thinking in US dollar terms, he thought it was too little, the equivalent of about US$100. In New York, even a single pomegranate would cost him not less than US$2. He gave it a thought and concluded that he had to add value to the pomegranates by doing something more and not just selling the fruit as they are. After discussing it with some local people he came to the conclusion that pomegranate juice was the best option and he decided to extract pomegranate juice and sell it in the market. He asked the manager to peel the pomegranates and extract the juice. The manager got hold of some local people and after working for the entire day they could only peel few pomegranates and only a few litres of juice was ready. Himanshu thought that this was a classic example of 'much cry, little wool'.

The Pomegranate Peeling Machine

He thought more about it and called his friend Rohan, who studied with him in engineering college and was now working as a researcher and had already been granted a number of patents for his inventions. Rohan assured him that he would work on a pomegranate peeling machine and email him the design and drawings. After working on it, Rohan and Himanshu were able to make a new pomegranate peeling machine which could peel two pomegranates a minute. This was too good. Both of them worked on the design further and added a juicer to the peeling machine. Now these machines could peel and extract juice from two pomegranates in a minute, which means more than a hundred pomegranates in an hour.

Himanshu kept this machine a closely guarded secret and worked on it himself and produced a lot of pomegranate juice which was now being sold in the local market. As his orchards were next to NH-8 and there was a bus stop, he set up a kiosk to sell pomegranate juice there. His business picked up and flourished day by day. He was very happy that he was able to apply his technical and management education to a real life situation. He was getting fantastic return on investment.

Patent for the Machine

Bhimsingh, the local landlord, owned almost double the area of pomegranate orchards that Himanshu did, and had tremendous political clout in the area. He was very powerful and the local people considered him to be their Godfather. He also lent money to the poor and needy, though he charged usurious rates of interest. Bhimsingh heard about Himanshu's flourishing business and was eager to establish a similar business for his pomegranate orchards. He talked to Himanshu about the machine and offered to buy one. Himanshu politely refused. Bhimsingh was not ready to accept no for an answer. He threatened Himanshu with dire consequences, to which Himanshu did not pay any attention. However, Himanshu was disturbed and told Rohan about the incident. Rohan suggested to immediately file for a patent for the machine, which Himanshu did the next week. His patent agent assured him it was possible as the machine was new and no one had thought about it earlier.

P8 and the Slogan

Himanshu paid more attention to his business and came up with a banner at the kiosk that said 'fresh pomegranate juice is available'. He also made up his mind to brand the pomegranate juice. He brainstormed and came up with a very simple name, 'P8', which was inspired by the language used in SMS. 'P' was the first letter of pomegranate and '8' was the last syllable of the word pomegranate. Later, he applied for trademark registration for 'P8'. Meanwhile, he wrote 'TM' after 'P8' to convey that it was his trademark and no one should use it. Once he got the registration for the trademark, he would start using an 'R' in a circle, ®, to denote that the trademark had been registered. While writing an SMS, it is common to write 'Gr8' for 'great', so, Himanshu came up with the slogan, 'P8 is Gr8, Drink P8' and in Hindi he wrote '*P8 piyo, mast jiyo*', meaning 'drink P8 and enjoy life'. He immediately wrote a 'C' in a circle, ©, to denote that he had copyrighted the slogans. He contacted and paid local singers to set this jingle to music which was later broadcast regularly at the local FM Radio Station. He also started a website, 'p8.com', and registered the domain name with ICANN. Now his business was well known, not only in Anarabad but also in India and through his social networking sites and all his friends and relatives all over the world. He also advertised the trademark P8 and slogans in the national and local dailies.

Shelf Life

The only problem Himanshu was facing was that the shelf life of the juice was short and hence it was not possible to extract much pomegranate juice and store it. He discussed this matter with Rohan, who promised to find a suitable chemical which could be added as a preservative without having an adverse effect on its taste. Rohan visited Anarabad and they worked in a make-shift laboratory for a couple of weeks and were successful in finding the preservative ABC, which was well suited for pomegranate juice and extended the shelf-life to about six months. They filed another application with the patent office for patenting the preservative. Himanshu installed more machines and was now able to extract a large quantity of pomegranate juice, pack it with preservatives and sell the juice to a large number of customers. The business was booming and he was very happy with this development.

Competitor Replicates

Bhimsingh was always jealous of Himanshu's success, and now he was hell-bent on ruining Himanshu's business. He got a peeling and juice extracting machine from the local grey market which was a slavish reproduction of Himanshu's patented machine and started copying Himanshu's business model. With his local connections, political clout and social position, Bhimsingh was able to expand his business, poach Himanshu's employees and get supply contracts for pomegranate juice to government offices. There was a definite negative impact on Himanshu's business. One evening Himanshu's manager came with a long face and informed him that their warehouses were full of pomegranate juice packets and there was almost no sales. Himanshu was very disappointed and frustrated.

The Secret Herbs

In such a situation, Himanshu always remembered his mother who never failed to give him courage, strength and emotional support. He called her, and she told him that there was nothing to worry about. She would reach Anarabad the next day and tell him a little secret of making pomegranate juice tastier. Next day she reached Anarabad and gave him some herbs and told him to mix a pinch of those herbs in a fine powder form in a glass of pomegranate juice. When Himanshu tasted it, he found that the taste had enhanced amazingly. His mother cautioned him that this was a secret and only Himanshu should mix these herbs in the juice and should not tell anyone else about it. Himanshu promised to do so. Thus, the mixing of these herbs became a 'trade secret' for his business. P8 launched it as a new, improved flavour and named it 'P8–Magic'. It was well received by the customers and got rave reviews in print and electronic media. It was a U-turn for his business. Customers almost queued up to buy P8-Magic. There was no looking back. The business just grew and grew.

The Cup

Encouraged by recent success, Himanshu asked one of his designer friends to design a new cup in the shape of pomegranate. His friend designed it beautifully as a red pomegranate with the handle in the shape of numeral '8'. The design was a treat for the eyes. Himanshu filed for a design registration for the cup. His customers, particularly children, were now fond of buying these cups—both to enjoy the juice and thereafter to keep the cup with them as a souvenir. This design became very famous. The cup also had a fantastic label which was artistically made by

Gagan—an extremely talented student at the Art College in Mumbai. The label exhibited a striking colour combination of red with a yellow background, depicting pomegranates in a string on the border and the slogan 'P8 is Gr8, Drink P8' and in Hindi '*P8 piyo, mast jiyo*'. Himanshu had engaged Gagan on a contractual basis, paid him for his services and made it very clear in the contract that Gagan had transferred all rights for the artistic work to Himanshu. It also mentioned that Anarabad has a Geographical Indication registration for pomegranates. Himanshu got a copyright for the label as soon as it was completed and transferred it to him. However, to have better protection and the best prima facie evidence, he filed an application to register it as a copyright. He was contemplating to file applications to get trademark protection also for the shape of the cup, the slogans—both in English and in Hindi, and the entire packaging including the label and colour combination.

2

Patents

If a man can write a better book, preach a better sermon, or make a better mouse-trap, than his neighbour, though he built his house in the woods, the world will make a beaten path to his door.

Ralph Waldo Emerson

Historically, patents are the most important branch of intellectual property responsible for the economic development. Some writers go to the extent of writing that the economic development of the United States in the last one and a half century is the development of US patent law. Patents are rights created by statute—negative rights that stop everyone except the inventor from benefitting from the invention. It has to be the inventor who is rewarded by the society. As this protection is provided by the enacted law, it depends on the jurisdiction in which the invention has been made and needs to be protected.

SALIENT FEATURES

Patent law creates a limited monopoly to encourage inventors to create new processes, machines, products or improve on existing things for benefit of the public. After the expiry of the patent, the invention is freely available to everyone. To obtain such a patent the inventor must apply to the concerned patent office specifying the requirements of the patent law, namely, patentable subject matter, novelty, non-obviousness and usefulness. Besides these four, the inventor must enable the public to make and use the invention. The term of a patent is twenty years. Patents enrich public knowledge by adding new knowledge. The patentee gets exclusive rights to make use of, sell, licence or assign the patent. The inventor must be vigilant to file for the patent shortly after disclosing the patent to the public or after publishing it. In case there is a very long delay in filing the patent application the inventor may lose the right to a patent. Getting a patent is an expensive proposition, as the inventor has to incur the filing cost, fees to the patent attorney, etc. Later costs to protect the patent from infringement litigation may also be quite high. The benefits of a patent are primarily exclusive rights, which may be commercially exploited. One important thing to be kept in mind—patents can only be granted for an invention, not a discovery. A discovery is finding something which already exists and which is found by effort or by chance whereas an invention takes place when the inventor creates something by thinking about an idea and by application of intellect. Thus, a patent shall not be granted for anything where there is complete or partial prior knowledge about it.

HISTORICAL PERSPECTIVE

Some writers go back to Aristotle's *Politics*, composed in the fourth century BC to record the first reference to patents, however, it is an isolated reference. The first real system was established in Venice in the late fifteenth century by the Venetian Senate's 1474 Act, which provided for a ten-year patent term.

The United Kingdom

Patents came to England sometime in the middle of the sixteenth century and were later formalised by the Statute of Monopolies of 1624, which was a unique combination of competition (anti-trust) law and patent protection and provided for a fourteen-year patent term. There was not much activity on the patents front in the seventeenth century. It was only after the Industrial Revolution that patents came back into focus. The applicant for a patent was made to provide a sufficient description of his invention by the celebrated judgment in *Liardet* v. *Johnson* (1778) by Lord Mansfield. This was the inventor's contribution to society in exchange for patent protection, which became almost synonymous to litigation. James Watt and Matthew Boulton earned a lot of money with their steam engine, built in England during the Industrial Revolution, but with money came protracted litigation, *Boulton* v. *Bull* (1795) and *Hornblower* v. *Boulton* (1799). The patent system was reformed in 1852, which led to an increase in patenting activity. 1883 saw more reforms with a modern Patent Office, and in 1905, adoption of better search methods which looked into inventions made in the last fifty years. Nothing dramatic happened until the 1970s, when an international patent system came into existence. The Patent Cooperation Treaty (PCT, Washington, 1970) was put into effect in 1978.

The United States

The first US patent statute—the Patent Act of 1790—was passed in May 1790 and the first patent was issued to Samuel Hopkins of Pittsford, Vermont, for a process for making potash from wood ashes. The patent system was thoroughly revised in 1836 when a formal system of examination was introduced. Thereafter, the patent system grew phenomenally and landmark patents were granted during that period—electric bulb, telephone, automobile, etc. The period between the First World War and the Second World War, roughly speaking, demonstrated weaker protection. The 1952 Patent Act signalled going back to strong protection. Getting a patent became easy in the absence of rigorous examination and it led to lesser importance being given by the industry to patents. The patent system received an impetus with the creation of the new Court of Appeals for the Federal Circuit (CAFC) in 1982. Patents grew by leaps and bounds and of late the pendulum seems to have swung in the other direction: the general mood is that there is too much patent protection.

India

The first law made in India with regard to patents was in 1856 and was based on the British Patent Law of 1852. In this act, the inventor or trader was granted 'exclusive privileges' for a period of fourteen years. New laws were enacted in quick succession in 1872, 1883 and 1888. Later, the Indian Patents and Designs Act, 1911, replaced all previous laws. After Independence, the Patents Act, 1970, was enacted as per the changing aspirations of the people of India and the changing times. There was a demand for affordable medical care and medicines in a poor country of millions. The new law allowed only process patents for pharmaceuticals, opening the door for reverse-engineering of foreign medicines by Indian companies.

The 1970 Act was brought into force on April 20, 1972, with publication of the Patent Rules, 1972. Post TRIPS, the 1970 Act was amended in 1999 with retrospective effect from January 1,

1995. It provided provisions relating to filing applications for product patents in the areas of pharmaceuticals and agro-chemicals. The 1970 Act was again amended in 2002, and again in 2005, which inter alia allowed product patents in pharmaceuticals and came into force on January 1, 2005.

Internationalization

Besides the Patent Cooperation Treaty of 1970, efforts have been made through the World Trade Organization (WTO, 1995). India is a signatory of the WTO and also the Agreement on Trade-Related Aspects of Intellectual Property Rights (TRIPS), an integral part of the WTO.

ESSENTIAL CONDITIONS

For the grant of a patent the following conditions are essential:

- ▶ Novelty
- ▶ Non-obviousness
- ▶ Utility
- ▶ Enablement

Novelty

Means that the invention must be new and not known to the world. So, if you invent the wheel, you are sure not to be granted a patent for it. Thus the commonly used phrase 'reinventing the wheel'. To receive a patent, one has to make something new, something better. I began the chapter with the famous words about the mouse-trap by the celebrated American essayist, poet and philosopher, Ralph Waldo Emerson.

Non-obviousness

Means that there must be an inventive step which has not been obvious to any person trained in that particular field. It must be a valuable contribution to society that no one thought of before.

Utility

Means that the invention must be of some use. This includes general utility, specific utility or moral utility. Patents are granted by specific jurisdiction and, hence, it depends on the laws in that jurisdiction as to what may be regarded as utility. New contraceptives in countries which regard any birth-control mechanism as illegal shall never be granted a patent in that country. The same invention may be welcome and granted a patent in a country that allows birth-control. The same applies to gambling machines and other gadgets. Thus, the invention must be legal and promote activities which are *interpreted as legal* by the law of that land.

Enablement

Means providing sufficient and detailed information about the invention so that any appropriately trained person is able to make it. It goes without saying that the inventor must make the invention. There can be no patent granted merely for the concept or idea. It has to be operational.

PRIOR ART, PUBLIC DOMAIN, PUBLIC USE

The most important criterion for the award of a patent is novelty, which has to be understood in conjunction with prior art— something which is already known to mankind. Anything which is already known in general or to a specific group of persons, whether in the same country or abroad, cannot be patented. The simple reason is that the so-called inventor has not invented anything and it is merely a transferer of knowledge from one place to another, or from a small group of persons to the larger community. Society would surely not like to award a so-called inventor with exclusive rights for a definite period of time. Moreover, if the inventor had really invented something new and did not bother to apply for a patent within a reasonable period of time, there is a good chance that such an invention may be termed as 'prior art' or 'public use'. Hence, it is of utmost importance to apply for a patent the day the invention is made and the papers are ready. Edison followed this conscientiously and had more than 1000 patents in his name.

A recent case decided by the Madras High Court highlights the point well.

S Paul Raj versus TCS (Tata Consultancy Services)[1]

S Paul Raj, a BSc student (Computer Science) came up with the concept named 'FLYGUARD', which involved retaining all data—physiological and physical—of a traveller on magnetic tape. It included the place of origin, fingerprints, retinal/corneal pictures and other details, which would be stored on a main processor. Such details would be made available to all government agencies from a network. He did not operationalize the idea. Instead, he wished to sell it to TCS for Rs 5 crores so that it could be developed further and put to good commercial use. In 2007, he filed an application at the Patent Office for FLYGUARD.

Later, he found his innovation on the TCS webpage as 'ePassport (Smartcard)' and also as 'TCS ePassport Solution'. He filed a petition in the Madras High Court seeking injunction, to which TCS replied that the process of flying across countries using a digitally encrypted biometric card embodying physical and physiological parameters and doing away with the requirement of passport or visa was bereft of any novelty. It was neither original nor new. Such a concept involved technologies that had already been in the public domain for a long time. Moreover, the idea itself was not patentable, as the practical application or discovery that leads to patentability was absent.

The Madras High Court dismissed his case in 2009 on the grounds that it was an attempt to coerce TCS to extract certain privileges and amounts on the basis of the so-called invention, otherwise available in public domain.

Blending Chalk with Cheese

An inventor comes up with the idea of using a jug to pour orange juice and claims that it is a new use of a jug and hence he should be granted a patent. The claim itself makes one laugh. Similarly, a so-called inventor claims to have invented glass noodles—as contradistinguished with cup noodles—and bowl noodles and beaker noodles. Does he deserve to be granted a patent? The reply is a big NO. These are not acceptable as patents as they are quite obvious. However, things which are not obvious will surely be considered. This includes things which generally do not go together. It is well known that when lime juice is mixed with hot milk, the milk curdles. A chef invents a potion which contains a mixture of lime juice and hot milk in such a proportion that milk does not curdle. Moreover, the shelf life of milk increases ten times and it becomes more delicious and nutritious. He claims to have invented the process which makes it possible. In such a scenario, the invention shall be considered, provided other essential conditions are fulfilled.

PHOSITA

Any new development, inventive step or innovation in making an improved automobile engine or instruments used for cardiac surgery may not be obvious to the layman. However, those improvements may be quite obvious to the expert in that particular field. The test for obviousness is thus: *the invention must not be obvious to a PHOSITA*, or, 'Person Having Ordinary Skill In the Art'. There should be an 'inventive step'. As patents can be sought for major, as well as minor, inventions, there needs to be clarity about what is a minor invention and hence obvious to the PHOSITA. Patent laws developed in different jurisdictions, independently resulting in variations, are regarded as the inventive step.

INVENTIVE STEP AND FLASH OF CREATIVE GENIUS

In the *Cuno*[2] case in 1941, the American Supreme Court held that '[T]he new device, however, useful it may be, must reveal the *flash of creative genius, not merely the skill of the calling*.' This was made a statutory expression as section 103 in the 1952 Act in the US.

The inventive step has also been an important criterion in England. Lord Justice Oliver[3] identified four stages to determine the inventive step:

(1) The court must identify the inventive concept embodied in the patent.
(2) It must assume the mantle of the normally skilled but unimaginative addressee in the art at the priority date and impute to him what was, at that date, common general knowledge in the art in question.

(3) It must identify what, if any, differences exist between the matters cited as being 'known or used' and the alleged invention.

(4) It must ask itself whether, viewed without any knowledge of the alleged invention, those differences constituted steps which would have been obvious to the skilled man or whether they required any degree of invention.

PATENT PROTECTION AND EXPENSIVE LEGAL BATTLES

Patents do not come cheap. Filing for a patent and protecting a patent are expensive propositions. It is a business decision which requires careful analysis of the legal environment prevailing in the country. Edison found it conducive to fight a long legal battle to protect his electric bulb as the legal environment in the United States for protection of patents was highly evolved in the late nineteenth century. Let us have a look at the landmark case of Edison's bulb, decided by the US Supreme Court in 1895.

Edison's bulb[4]

Thomas Edison once commented, 'My electric light inventions have brought me no profits, only forty years of litigation.' Edison spent more than US$2 million in the late 1800s in patent litigation for the bulb.

There was a significant legal battle between Sawyer and Man and the Edison systems of electric lighting. Sawyer and Man's lamp consisted of an incandescing conductor of carbon made from a vegetable, fibrous material, in contradistinction to a similar conductor made from mineral or gas carbon, and also in the form of a conductor made from such vegetable carbon. The experiments with carbonized paper and wood carbon were imperfectly successful and the lamp was never a commercial success. A patent was, however, granted for this lamp.

Edison's lamp consisted of a burner made of carbonized bamboo of a particular quality. It was about six inches long, 5/1000 of an inch thick and had electrical resistance of more than 100 ohms. It was bent into the form of a loop and the ends were secured to two fine platinum wires, which passed through a glass stem. A glass globe was fused to the glass stem. Edison worked very hard to identify the right carbonized bamboo. Edison tried as many as thirty or forty different woods of exogenous growth and ultimately found a bamboo grown in Japan to have the particular characteristics suitable for a filament, as fibres ran nearly parallel than in other species of wood.

Sawyer and Man filed a case against Edison for infringing the patent—using a conductor made from a vegetable, fibrous material. The US Supreme Court decided in 1895 that Sawyer and Man did not have a monopoly over all fibrous and textile materials for incandescent conductors. An examination of over 6,000 vegetable growths showed that none of them possessed the qualities that fitted them for that purpose. The Court held that Sawyer and Man had made a very broad claim covering all fibrous and textile materials, which was not justified.

USING PATENTS AS A LETHAL WEAPON IN BUSINESS STRATEGY

As the patent regime in India is becoming stronger, Indian companies are using patents as an essential tool and, at times, as a weapon in their business strategy. The recent case of Bajaj versus

TVS is an apt illustration. The matter has still not been finally decided by the courts, but the interim orders created the desired effect for both companies. Let us discuss the case.

Bajaj versus TVS[5]

Bajaj Auto Limited filed a patent application in 2002 for 'An Improved Internal Combustion Engine Working on Four Stroke Principle', which was granted in 2005 as Indian Patent No. 195904. The invention used two spark plugs for efficient burning of lean air fuel mixture in a small bore engine between 45 and 70 millimetres, which resulted in better combustion in a comparatively shorter time leading to emission reduction and improved fuel consumption while maintaining the predetermined level of performance. The use of two spark plugs in large bore engines or in high performance/racing bikes was already known in the automobile industry. In cases of racing applications, twin plugs have been applied in small bore air cooled engines which are not lean burn.

These engines used twin plugs as a means of mitigating knock, which also gave added reliability by preventing loss of ignition/misfire. This invention, 'DTS-i Technology', of providing a second spark plug in a small bore engine running lean, was never thought of or implemented in the automobile industry. Bajaj started using DTS-i Technology in its motorcycles in 2003.

TVS Motor Company Limited launched motor bikes of 125-CC in December 2007 under the trade mark 'FLAME' powered with a lean burn internal combustion engine of bore size 54.5 millimetres with a twin spark plug configuration. Bajaj sued TVS on the grounds that its patent was infringed upon and sought a permanent injunction. TVS argued that Bajaj's so-called invention was already known as the US Honda patent No. 4534322 dated August 13, 1985, and also suffered from the 'vice of obviousness'. Bajaj reiterated that its invention was not obvious and the Honda patent was neither in respect of small bore engine nor aimed at efficient combustion of lean mixture.

TVS suffered a big blow when, the Madras High Court (Single-Judge Bench) granted a temporary injunction in February 2008. The Madras High Court, however, did not decide the dispute regarding the validity of the patent. Later, the Division Bench of the Madras High Court granted relief in favour of TVS in May 2009. The Supreme Court in Bajaj's appeal directed the dispute regarding patent to be decided expeditiously by the Madras High Court and allowed TVS, in the meantime, to sell its motor bike FLAME while maintaining accurate accounts of sales.

More than a century ago, Henry Ford used patent law in the United States to call George Selden's bluff and took the bold step of promising to indemnify Ford's customers. The rest is history. Let us read a little bit about the friendship between Edison and Ford before discussing the car and Selden patent.

Edison–Ford Friendship

Henry Ford was introduced to Thomas Edison in 1896 as 'a young fellow who has made a gas car'. Edison, by that time was a legend with more than 1000 patented inventions, asked Henry some questions and banged his fist down on the table to emphasize his satisfaction. 'Young man,' he said, 'that's the thing! You have it! Your car is self contained and carries its own power plant.' And thus began a long friendship. To celebrate the fiftieth anniversary of the light bulb, Ford established the Edison Institute in 1929. Invention of the first successful incandescent bulb in the original

Menlo Park laboratory was enacted. Ford paid attention to the minutest details for accuracy. Edison remarked that Ford got everything 99-9/10ths perfect. The inaccuracy, he told Ford, was that 'our floor was never this clean.' Later, at the banquet, Edison said, 'I can only say that in the fullest meaning of the term, he is my friend.'

Surely, the legendary patentee's confidence must have rubbed off on Ford to give him tremendous courage to fight it out with George Selden.

Ford–Selden patent litigation

George Selden, a patent attorney from Rochester, New York, was granted a patent in 1895 for a 'road engine' which was a three-cylinder motor vehicle. Selden collected royalties from all American car manufacturers, who got patent licensing rights to build cars. Ironically, Selden had never built a car and was unabashedly enjoying patent benefits in the name of the 'Association of Licensed Automotive Manufacturers' (ALAM), his holding company.

When Henry Ford, encouraged by Edison's words, made up his mind to make an inexpensive car for the masses, refused to pay royalties to Selden and thus infringe the patent, Selden took Ford to court for a long legal battle and also took out magazine advertisements.

NOTICE

To Manufacturers, Dealers, Importers, Agents, and Users of Gasoline Automobiles

United States Letters Patent, No. 549160, granted to George B Selden, November 5, 1895, controls broadly all gasoline

---

automobiles which are accepted as commercially practical. Licenses under this patent have been secured from the owners by the following named manufacturers and importers:

- *names of twenty eight companies*

These manufacturers are pioneers in this industry, and have commercialized the gasoline vehicle by many years of development and at great cost. They are the owners of upward of 400 United States Patents, covering many of the most important improvements and details of manufacture. Both the basic Selden patent and all other patents owned as aforesaid will be enforced against all infringers.

No other manufacturers or importers are authorized to make or sell gasoline automobiles, and any person making, selling, or using such machines made or sold by any unlicensed manufacturers or importers, will be liable to prosecution for infringement.

Source: Association of Licensed Automobile Manufacturers, New York

Ford countered with his own advertisements.

NOTICE

To Dealers, Importers, Agents, and Users of our Gasoline Automobiles

We will protect you against any prosecution for alleged infringements of patents. Regarding alleged infringement of the Selden patent, we beg to quote the well-known Patent Attorneys, Messrs Parker & Burton: 'The Selden patent is not a broad one, and if it was, it is anticipated. It does not cover a practicable machine, no practicable machine can be made from it, and never was, so far as we can ascertain. It relates to that form of carriage called a FORE CARRIAGE. None of that type have ever been in use; all have been failures.' 'No court in the United States has ever decided in favour of the patent on the merits of the case; all it has ever done was to record a prior agreement between the parties.'

We are the pioneers of the GASOLINE AUTOMOBILE. Our Mr Ford made the first Gasoline Automobile in Detroit, and the third in the United States. His machine, built in 1893, two years prior to the issue of the Selden patents November 5, 1895, is still in use. Our Mr Ford also built the famous '999' Gasoline Automobile, which was driven by Barney Oldfield in New York on July 25, 1903, a mile in 55 4/5 seconds, on a circular track, which is the world's record.

Mr Ford, driving his own machine, beat Mr Winton at Grosse Pointe track in 1901. We have always been winners.

Source: Ford Motor Company, Detroit, Michigan.

Selden's patent was upheld at the trial court. Ford took the risk and appealed. Selden's patent was overturned in 1911. Ford had the last laugh. This is a fantastic illustration about enablement. Any inventor who cannot make his own invention work can never be granted a patent. In case, he is granted a patent, it is sure to be revoked, if challenged.

INTENTION TO ABANDON AND CONTROL

An inventor must keep control over his invention and related proceedings until a patent is granted. He cannot afford to be lackadaisical about it, which is regarded as abandoning it. It would be interesting to go through the following two cases—Ericsson in India in 2010 and Nicholson's Pavement patent in the United States in 1877.

Ericsson[6]

The Swedish company Ericsson filed a patent application in July 2005 for an invention 'A Method and Apparatus for Supporting Content Purchases Over a Public Communication Network.' The Patent Office was examining the application and Ericsson was responding to queries raised. In October 2008, Ericsson received a letter from the Patent Office that the application was not in order and the last date to put the application in order had expired and, therefore, 'the application is deemed to have been abandoned.' Ericsson was shocked.

It filed a petition in the Delhi High Court with the grievance that it was religiously responding to the queries of the Patent Office and that it had not abandoned the application. Also, natural justice demands that it should have been given a chance to explain prior to abandoning the application.

The Court allowed the petition and reasoned that where in response to an examination report, an applicant does nothing by way of meeting the objections raised therein within the time stipulated, and does not seek extension of time for that purpose only then it can be said that such application should be 'deemed to have been abandoned'. It also held that 'abandonment requires a conscious act on the part of the applicant which would manifest the *intention to abandon* the application.'

This case can very well be compared with the Nicholson's case in the City of Elizabeth. Nicholson's patent was upheld by the US Supreme Court primarily because during the experimental use by the public, he never let things go out of his control. He, thus, never *abandoned* his invention.

Nicholson's Pavement Patent[7]

Samuel Nicholson was granted a patent in 1867 for a new and improved wooden pavement. Streets and roadways faced the problems of horses' feet slipping (due to rain, snow and sleet), too much noise, unequal wear, and the rotting and sinking away of earth from below. Nicholson's pavement took care of these problems and was also easy to construct, cheap and durable. The pavement Nicholson put down by way of experiment was publicly used for about six years before he filed an application for a patent.

The City of Elizabeth, New Jersey entered into a contract with the New Jersey Wood-Paving Company for construction of pavement in the city. The company used Nicholson's patented method for construction without paying royalties to him. Nicholson sued the company and the City of Elizabeth. The matter finally reached the US Supreme Court.

One of the essential conditions to be granted a patent is that the invention should be new and a natural corollary is that it should not have been in public use. The New Jersey Wood-Paving Company argued in the court that Nicholson's invention was known to the world for about six years as it was in public use and thus, the patent was invalid. Nicholson claimed that he was experimenting; the invention was not in public use and hence the patent was valid.

Nicholson never intended to abandon his right to a patent. According to a toll-collector, 'Mr Nicholson was there almost daily, and when he came he would examine the pavement, would often walk over it, cane in hand, striking it with his cane, and making particular examination of its condition.' In 1877, the Supreme Court upheld the patent and remarked that, 'the nature of street pavement is such that it cannot be experimented upon satisfactorily except on a highway, which is always public.'

DISPUTE RESOLUTION

With more and more countries joining hands for patent protection globally, technology is being transferred much more freely between companies from different countries, resulting in the need to define clearly at the outset as to how future disputes need to be resolved. Cases lacking clarity may often result in unending litigation in foreign courts which is surely a drain on time, effort, and money. It also creates avoidable uncertainty. Let us examine the case of well-known companies, Philips from The Netherlands, 3M from the United States, and Moser Baer from India.

Moser Baer, Philips, and 3M[8]

Moser Baer India Ltd entered into six Disc Patent Licence Agreements (DPLAs) with Philips between 2001 and 2003. Philips licensed its patents in respect of the following types of discs: CD-R, CD-RW, DVD+R, DVD-R, DVD-RW, and DVD+RW. The DPLAs were for ten years and inter alia mentioned the quantum of royalty payable by Moser Baer to Philips. Both the parties agreed to the jurisdiction of the competent Courts at The Hague, The Netherlands.

In 1995, Philips had entered into a Cross License Agreement (CLA) with Minnesota Mining and Manufacturing Company (3M) and agreed to reciprocal, royalty free licences for each other's patents relating to optical disc technology. 3M assigned its rights to the Imation Corporation. Moser Baer India Ltd sold discs to Imation and its subsidiary 'Global Data Media' and did not pay royalties to Philips. Moser Baer and Imation argued that the sale was covered under the CLA to which Philips did not agree. A dispute arose.

Philips filed a case in the competent court at The Hague and Imation filed a case at the Minnesota District Court. Philips claimed US$655 million from Moser Baer. Meanwhile, Imation and Philips agreed to negotiate and resolved the dispute. After several rounds, settlement talks broke down. Moser Baer filed a case in the Delhi High Court, praying that the dispute be resolved in Delhi as the proceedings at The Hague and Minnesota would entail enormous amounts of time, effort and money. Philips insisted that the Delhi High Court had no jurisdiction and the matter had to be resolved in the court at The Hague. In 2008, the Delhi High Court held that as per the DPLA, it has no jurisdiction in the matter and it must be decided by the court at The Hague.

This decision has been a shot in the arm for patent licencing agreements and paves the way for smooth transfers of technology. It is significant for certain foreign patent holders, who are a bit unsure about the time taken in courts in India, and thus shy away from even initiating a dialogue for technology transfer.

BUSINESS METHOD PATENTS

Being granted a patent for a new method for doing business is not an old phenomenon. It started in the US in 1998 with the State Street Bank case. In India it is not accepted for patenting.

State Street Bank & Trust Co v. Signature Financial Group (1998)

Signature Financial Group is the assignee of the United States Patent No. 5193056 which is entitled 'Data Processing System for Hub and Spoke Financial Services Configuration'. The patent was issued to Signature on March 9, 1993. The patent is generally directed to a data processing system for implementing an investment structure which was developed for use in Signature's business as an administrator and accounting agent for mutual funds. The system facilitates a structure whereby mutual funds (Spokes) pool their assets in an investment portfolio (Hub) organized as a partnership. This configuration provides the administrator of a mutual fund with the advantageous combination of economies of scale in administering investments coupled with the tax advantages of a partnership.

State Street Bank (SSB) and Signature are both in the business of acting as custodians and accounting agents for multi-tiered partnership fund financial services. SSB negotiated with Signature for a licence to use its patented data processing system however, the negotiations failed. SSB later moved the court, asserting invalidity and unenforceability of Signature's patent on the ground that the patent failed to satisfy the test of statutory subject matter as it was a business method patent.

The United State's Court of Appeals for the Federal Circuit looked into the matter and found that the system allowed for the allocation among the spokes of the hub's daily income, expenses, and net realized and unrealized gain or loss, calculating each day's total investments based on the concept of a book capital account. This enabled the determination of a true asset value of each spoke and accurate calculation of allocation ratios between or among the spokes. The system also tracked all the relevant data determined on a daily basis for the hub and each spoke, so that aggregate year-end income, expenses, and capital gain or loss could be determined for accounting and tax purposes for the hub and, as a result, for each publicly traded spoke. These calculations were performed quickly and accurately. A mutual fund administrator, for instance, is required to calculate the value of the shares to the nearest penny within as little as an hour and a half after the market closes. As the calculations are very complex, it is necessary to use a computer to perform the task. Signature's process allowed this task to be performed by a computer.

The US Supreme Court had identified three categories of subject matter that are unpatentable namely; laws of nature, natural phenomena, and abstract ideas. The Court later held that mathematical algorithms were not patentable subject matter to the extent that they were merely abstract ideas. The Court of Appeals, however, held that Signature's patent was a valid patent. It held,

> 'Today, we hold that the transformation of data, representing discrete dollar amounts, by a machine through a series of mathematical calculations into a final share price, constitutes a practical application of a mathematical algorithm, formula, or calculation, because it produces "a useful, concrete and tangible result"—a final share price momentarily fixed for recording and reporting purposes and even accepted and relied upon by regulatory authorities and in subsequent trades.'

The Business Method Exception

The Court also talked about the judicially-created, so-called 'business method' exception to statutory subject matter. The Court held that since its inception the business method exception has merely represented the application of some general but no longer applicable legal principle, perhaps arising out of the 'requirement for invention'.

The court cited Judge Newman (Schrader, Federal Circuit, 1994) who had categorically rubbished the creation of a new category of 'business method' exception in the following words:

> 'The business method exception is...an unwarranted encumbrance to the definition of statutory subject matter in section 101, that should be discarded as error-prone, redundant, and obsolete. It

merits retirement from the glossary of section 101... All of the "doing business" cases could have been decided using the clearer concepts of Title 35. Patentability does not turn on whether the claimed method does "business" instead of something else, but on whether the method, viewed as a whole, meets the requirements of patentability as set forth in Sections 102, 103, and 112 of the Patent Act'.

The Court of Appeals added in the latter part of the judgment that the patent office personnel have had difficulty in properly treating claims directed to methods of doing business and hence, claims should not be categorized as methods of doing business. Instead such claims should be treated like any other process claims.

This judgment opened the floodgates for business method patents in the US and thousands of business method patents have been granted in the last decade. Initially, there were nascent Internet companies that tried to get exclusive rights to specific types of online transactions. Later, however, more established companies tried their best to include the business method patents in their portfolios. These companies included IBM, Merrill Lynch, Amazon, Accenture, etc. Highly reputed companies were in a race to get as many business method patents as possible. Some investment firms also got business method patents for financial products. Such was the explosion in business method patent filings that it became quite difficult for the patent office to examine applications.

Another case—*Bilski* v. *Kappos*—reached the Court of Appeals after a decade, and this time the court, well aware of the changing situation, opined that explosion in business method patents was not a very good idea. It went to the root of the matter and held that such patents were in the category of unpatentable subject matter. The court further said that the sole test should be the 'machine–or–transformation' test. The matter was finally heard in the US Supreme Court.

Bilski v. *Kappos* (US Supreme Court, June 28, 2010)

Bernard Bilski and Rand Warsaw invented the 'Energy Risk Management Method'. They claimed that the invention explained how commodities buyers and sellers in the energy market can protect, or hedge, against the risk of price changes. Their main claim was claim No.1, which described a series of steps instructing how to hedge risk. Another claim placed claim No.1 into a simple mathematical formula. Other claims explained how these concepts could be applied to allow energy suppliers and consumers to minimize risk resulting from fluctuations in market demand. The patent examiner rejected the application on the grounds that the invention was not implemented on a specific apparatus, but merely manipulated an abstract idea and solved a purely mathematical problem. This decision was affirmed by the Board of Patent Appeals and Interferences and later by the Federal Circuit, which relied upon the 'machine-or-transformation' test.

Machine-or-transformation test
The test says that the claim process can be patented only if (i) it is tied to a particular machine or apparatus, or (ii) it transforms a particular article into a different state or thing.

Against the decision of the Federal Circuit, the inventors appealed in the US Supreme Court. The Federal Circuit's decision had come at a time when the Supreme Court had already signalled that too many patents were being granted for inventions that were obvious. Experts commented that the Federal Circuit was reacting to the anti-patent trend in the Supreme Court. The business method patents had already been in existence for more than ten years and it was being felt that certain obvious patents e.g., 'one-click' patent to Amazon.com and a patent to an inventor for inventing a technique for lifting a box should never have been granted. The field of business method patents had been highly controversial which provided a grand success to the issuance of non-technical process patents. The Bilski matter was pending in the US Supreme Court for some time and big consulting and technology service firms were anxiously waiting for the decision.

The decision came on June 28, 2010, when the Supreme Court decided that the machine-or-transformation test is not the sole test for patent eligibility. It held that same test may be a useful and important investigative tool, however, it is not the sole test for deciding whether an invention is a patent eligible process. The Court mentioned in the judgment that Section 101 of the Patent Act specifies four independent categories of inventions that are patent eligible namely; processes, machines, manufactures and compositions of matter. By choosing such expansive terms, the US Congress plainly contemplated that patent laws would be given wide scope and 'ingenuity should receive a liberal encouragement'. Section 100(b)'s process definition may include some methods of doing business and the 'ordinary, contemporary, common meaning' of 'method' does not exclude business methods. Thus it would not be clear what a business method exception would sweep in and whether it would exclude technologies for conducting a business more efficiently.

Regarding this case, the Supreme Court held that the application was not categorically outside of Section 101. However, the inventors' idea of getting protection for the concept of hedging risk and the application of that concept to energy markets was not a process under Section 101. It was merely an attempt to obtain a patent for abstract ideas. Claim 1 explained the basic concept of hedging and Claim 4 reduced that concept to a mathematical formula. Remaining claims provided broad examples of how hedging can be used in commodities and energy markets and it was an attempt to patent the use of the abstract hedging idea and then instruct the use of well known random analysis techniques to help establish some input into the equation. Such things cannot be allowed to be patented. The Court did not define further what constitutes a patentable process. They did, however, clarify that nothing in the judgment should be read as endorsing the Federal Circuit's interpretations of State Street Bank's case. The Court also made it clear that the Federal Circuit was free to develop any other limiting criteria that further the Patent Act's purposes.

This is one of the long-awaited landmark judgments coming from the US Supreme Court. The judgment received a mixed response as it did not categorically say 'no' to business method patents in the US and at the same time upheld the Federal Circuit's decision in Bilski case. The question regarding business method patents has been left wide open and it is up to the understanding of businesses and lawyers as to how new processes—whether technological or not—can be granted protection under patent law. One thing, though, is very much certain—the court has held that business method patents are not excluded from the category of process and 'machine-or-transformation' is not the only test for a patent to be granted.

PHARMACEUTICALS AND PATENTS

Patents for pharmaceutical products has been one of the most contentious issues between developed and developing countries, and India has been in favour of liberal patent laws in the field of pharmaceutical products. Most of the developing and least developed countries find it too expensive to buy patented life-saving medicines from Western companies. However, these companies and their governments have been pushing hard to have strict protection. This constant tussle brings in issues of human rights, making reasonable profits, corporate governance, transparency, protectionism and ultimately the issue of sovereignty. Countries, even after signing the TRIPS agreement, have the freedom to issue 'compulsory licences' to companies relating to the manufacture of pharmaceutical products for export to countries with public health. India follows this and it has been included in the law to ensure that patented pharmaceutical products may be manufactured and exported to countries having insufficient or no manufacturing capacity in that sector. A compulsory licence can also be granted by the government if (i) reasonable requirements of the public with respect to the patented invention have not been satisfied, (ii) it is not available at a reasonably affordable price, or (iii) the patented invention has not worked in India.

Well-known global pharmaceutical companies have taken legal recourse against the patent regime in India. This is the trend of late and it is expected that more and more matters shall reach the judicial forums for redressal. Following are two such cases: Cipla and Novartis.

F. Hoffman-La Roche v. *Cipla* (Delhi High Court, 2008)

La Roche is a Swiss company and sells the tablet formulation of 'Erlotinib' under the trademark and name of Tarceva. Erlotinib is medically termed as 'Human Epidermal Growth Factor Type-1/ Epidermal Growth Factor Receptor (HER/EGFR) inhibitor'.

Invention of this molecule has been a major breakthrough and innovation in the treatment of cancer. It is used to destroy some types of cancer cells while causing little harm to normal human cells.

La Roche was granted an Indian patent No. 196774 on February 23, 2007, by the Controller General of Patents, Trademarks and Designs, New Delhi. Due to a Development Collaboration and Licencing Agreement, La Roche had a licence to use, sell and offer for sale, licenced products including the drug Erlotinib marketed as Tarceva. It was authorized to cause enforcement of any intellectual property rights for any of their products. It is actively engaged in the manufacture, marketing and sale of Tarceva in various countries including India and it introduced Tarceva in India in April 2006.

In December 2007 and January 2008, La Roche came to know from print and electronic media that Cipla—one of the biggest pharmaceutical companies in India—was planning to launch a generic version of Erlotinib in India and for exporting to various countries. La Roche filed a petition in the Delhi High Court seeking permanent injunction and damages.

La Roche stated in court that Erlotinib was developed after long, sustained and substantial research, and after incurring enormous expenditure for the tests, mandatorily conducted to establish its efficacy and safety. This innovation was duly protected under the patent law in India and no person except those authorized to exercise the legal rights associated with the patented drug can be allowed or permitted to copy/simulate and/or re-create it in any manner or in any other name. La Roche stated that Cipla was following an illegal course to offer a generic version of the patented drug; firstly, in an unlawful manner by infringing its legal rights, and secondly, in a manner that may pose a serious hazard to the lives of the patients. La Roche claimed that the sale of Tarceva in India were as high as Rs 13.2 crores.

Cipla, in its reply, submitted that it had applied for approval for its Erlotinib tablet in May 2007, which was granted that October. The Government of Goa had also approved the manufacturing of such tablets in various pack sizes of 30, 60, 100, 500, and 1000. It had been selling the product since December 2007 under the brand 'Erlocip'. Cipla alleged that La Roche had not filed the complete patent specification before the Delhi High Court and thus did not deserve any relief.

Cipla had also filed for revocation of the patent granted to La Roche on the grounds that the patent was invalid. It contended that the patent claim lacked an inventive step and the patent was liable to be revoked as Erlotinib, being a Quinazolin derivative, only seeks to improve from the prior, existing art. Such an improvement would be obvious for a person skilled in the art, as Quinazolin compounds are known to inhibit growth and proliferation of mammalian cells and have been linked to cancer. It also provided evidence of the existence of at least three European patents, which date back to 1993 that disclose Quinazolin derivatives. It submitted that under such circumstances, the patent office ought not to have granted a patent for Erlotinib. It alleged that La Roche's attempt to protect Erlotinib established that it was indulging in ever-greening, which is contrary to Indian public policy, against the statutory language of Section 3(d) of the Patents Act and in the context of the pharmaceutical industry against national interests.

Cipla also contended that the patent was non-working and La Roche did not manufacture the products in India. Moreover, the product was not easily available on a commercial scale in India due to its high pricing. A La Roche tablet costs Rs 4,800 whereas Cipla's equivalent tablet costs Rs 1,600. Thus, a month's dosage for a patient undergoing treatment for cancer is Rs 1.4 lakhs if administered La Roche's tablets whereas the equivalent for Cipla's tablet would be Rs 46,000. Cipla further stated that in the area of life-saving drugs, it is in the interest of the general public and patients suffering from diseases like cancer that medicines are made available at affordable prices.

In its rejoinder, La Roche submitted evidence showing the effectiveness of Tarceva and stated that Erlotinib was not a derivative of a known substance, and moreover, that Section 3(d) was not country specific and that the explanation is merely declaratory about the required inventive step necessary for patentability of any product. It claimed that the invention was novel, inventive and had industrial application. It was never used in India or elsewhere in the world before the date of patent. It agreed that originally, an application was made to the Patent Office in India for twenty seven claims. However, during the examination, the application was restricted to two claims, for which patents were granted.

It further contended that amendments to the Patents Act had deleted Section 5, which had specified that only methods or processes of manufacture are patentable for certain inventions, so as to allow product patent protection in all fields of technology including areas of foods, medicines and drugs. The compulsion for amendments to the act was primarily to introduce product patents for all inventions as mandated by the TRIPS Agreement. It is legislative will and a country's resolve to integrate with a global, patent-friendly regime that affords protection to inventions. Finally, it was decided that arguments raised regarding the comparative cost were dangerous and such an argument was not material as the lower price of an infringing drug is irrelevant in an action for infringement of a pharmaceutical patent.

After going through the arguments of both sides, the Court rejected the interim injunction application of La Roche and stated that the invention for which the patent application was made was obvious to the unimaginative person skilled in the art and it would cause irreparable injury to the public if injunction was granted, as the public would be deprived of Cipla's products which are far more affordable than that of La Roche's.

La Roche filed an appeal before the Division Bench of the Delhi High Court challenging the order of the Single Judge. On April 24, 2009, the Division Bench rejected the appeal on the following grounds—non-disclosure of facts regarding patent No. 196774, absence of a prima facie case, a justified challenge to the validity of the applied patent and that allowing the appeal would be against public interest.

Earlier in the Novartis case, the Madras High Court had held that the amendments made to Section 3(d) of the Patents Act were valid and legal. This was also a judgment where the Indian courts decided in favour of the legislative changes made in India on the grounds of public/national interest and rejected giving a liberal interpretation to improvements made in an existing substance or process.

Novartis (Madras High Court, 2007)

Novartis, a Swiss pharmaceutical company, was granted EMR (Exclusive Marketing Rights) in 2003 for the cancer drug Glivec. Novartis had applied for EMR in anticipation of the product patent regime that was due to come into effect in India on January 1, 2005. As Novartis got the EMR, it filed petitions in different courts and sought injunction against certain Indian pharmaceutical companies which were manufacturing a generic version of Glivec.

Novartis achieved partial success in getting injunction orders.

As India was under an international treaty obligation (TRIPS), it amended the Patents Act, 1970 to allow product patents in pharmaceuticals. Prior to this, only process patents were allowed, which made it possible for Indian pharmaceutical companies to reverse-engineer the final product, work around the patented process and manufacture with a new process. This mechanism allowed them to manufacture the generic version of patented drugs legally. Glivec was one of them. The generic versions were sold at a fraction of the price of the patented drug, thus providing access to inexpensive medicines for Indian patients. At times, these were also exported to certain countries, mostly poor and undeveloped. In a sense, it was a great service to humanity—providing medicines at affordable prices. However, plainly speaking, it was stealing the intellectual property of the pharmaceutical companies which had put in a lot of time, research and money in coming up with such innovative medicine.

Post amendment, Section 3(d) of the Patents Act, 1970 reads as follows:

> Section 3: What are not inventions—
> 3(d) the mere discovery of a new form of a known substance which does not result in the enhancement of the known efficacy of that substance or the mere discovery of any new property or new use for a known substance or of the mere use of a known process, machine or apparatus unless such known process results in a new product or employs at least one new reactant.
> *Explanation: For the purposes of this clause, salts, esters, ethers, polymorphs, metabolites, pure form, particle size, isomers, mixtures of isomers, complexes, combinations and other*

derivatives of known substance shall be considered to be the same substance, unless they differ significantly in properties with regard to efficacy.

Novartis applied for a product patent for Glivec. The application was rejected by the Patent Office and Novartis appealed the decision in the Madras High Court. It asked for reversal of the patent office's order and also asked that the amended Section 3(d) be declared as unconstitutional and a violation of India's obligation to TRIPS. By that time the IPAB (Intellectual Property Appellate Board) had been constituted and the Madras High Court transferred the first request regarding the reversal of patent office's order to the IPAB. Regarding the second, the High Court held that the amended Section 3(d) was not ultra vires the constitution. However, regarding violation of TRIPS, it held that the Court had no jurisdiction.

The case is a landmark judgment as it did not allow a patent for any *incremental* change. A patent can only be granted for *substantial* improvement. Whether the improvement is substantial or not is a matter of Patent Office discretion, which shall always be guided by national and public interest. Thus, providing access to inexpensive medicines remains the mantra for patent protection. It has been a big jolt to Novartis and other pharmaceutical MNCs, however, and there had been global condemnation of Novartis for such legal action. Human Rights groups and even some pharmaceutical companies joined in criticizing Novartis for taking the matter to the Madras High Court. Most of the companies were not in favour of antagonizing India—a huge market for their products—or being branded as being against access of inexpensive medicines to the poor and needy.

CONCLUSION

Patents provide a very strong protection and are one of the most important branches of intellectual property. To be granted a patent, the invention must be new, non-obvious, useful, and fully enabled. The inventor must pay complete attention to maintain control over the invention. Any slackness may result in either the competitor taking advantage or the invention being termed as abandoned. The legal environment determines whether businesses would like to take the matters to court or resolve it on the business battlefield. The US has been providing a favourable legal environment to inventors for a long time and India is also following suit as is evident from the increasing number of cases being filed in Indian courts. Patent protection requires tremendous effort but the benefits are also enormous.

FOOD FOR THOUGHT

In 1972, in the US, Chakrabarty, a microbiologist, filed a patent application, assigned to the General Electric Co. The application asserted thirty six claims related to his invention of a bacterium. This human-made, genetically engineered bacterium was capable of breaking down multiple components of crude oil, which is believed to have significant value for the treatment of oil spills. Should a patent be granted for 'products of nature' or living things? Was Chakrabarty granted the patent?

FILL IN THE BLANKS

i) _____, Utility, Non-obviousness and enablement are the essential conditions for grant of a patent.

ii) The test for utility of an invention _____ in different countries.

iii) The Federal Circuit rejected the _____ patent on the basis of 'machine-or-transformation' test.

TRUE OR FALSE

a) A patent can be granted for anything which is already known to the public.

b) An abstract idea cannot be patented.

c) Pharmaceutical companies in India have welcomed the amendments made in the Patents Act.

d) Intellectual Property protection is more important than human rights.

KEY TO FILL IN THE BLANKS

i)   Novelty
ii) Varies
iii) Bilski

TRUE FALSE

a) False
b) True
c) False
d) False

NOTES

1   *Bajaj* v. *TVS*, Supreme Court, September 16, 2009; *TVS* v. *Bajaj*, Madras High Court, May 18, 2009; *Bajaj* v. *TVS*, Madras High Court, February 16, 2008.

2   *Consolidated Electric Light Co.* v. *McKeesport Light Co.*, US Supreme Court, 159 US 465 (1895).

3   *Cuno Corp.* v. *Automatic Devices Corp.*, 314 US 84 (1941) at 91.

4   *Elizabeth* v. *Pavement Company*, 97 US 126 (1877).

5   *Moser Baer India Limited* v. *Koninklijke Philips Electronics N.V.*, Delhi High Court, April 22, 2008.

6   *S Paul Raj* v. *TCS*, Madras High Court, August 11, 2009.

7   *Telefonaktiebolaget LM Ericsson (PUBL)* v. *Union of India*, Delhi High Court, March 11, 2010.

8   *Windsurfing International* v. *Tabur Marine*, R P C 59 (1985).

3

Copyrights

You must have surely heard the famous song *'Yeh chand sa roshan chehra, zulfon ka rang sunahra...'* sung by Mohd Rafi with Shammi Kapoor dancing on a boat on Dal Lake from the movie *Kashmir Ki Kali* released in 1964. In this song, the face of the beloved—Sharmila Tagore—has been compared to the moon. For a moment, let us assume that the idea of comparing the face of one's beloved is protected by intellectual property law, particularly copyright law. In such a scenario, no other person would be allowed by law to compare the face of his beloved to the moon. There would not have been any other song referring to *mehbooba, chand,* etc. It would have been a loss to Bollywood films. Fortunately, this is not the legal reality. The law says that only the 'expression' can be protected by copyright and that is why we have scores of songs with reference to *chand* including the film *Himalaya Ki God Mein,* released in 1965—just a year after *Kashmir Ki Kali*—with the famous song, *'Chand si mehbooba ho meri kab aisa maine socha tha...'* sung by Mukesh with Manoj Kumar wooing Mala Sinha on the silver screen.

SALIENT FEATURES

Copyright law covers a broad range of literary and artistic work which includes books, films, paintings, photographs, music, poetry, dance, drama, computer software, articles, journals, etc. Copyright protection is provided for the expression of an idea, but the idea itself is not protected. Thus a similar idea may be expressed in a number of ways and each expression will receive copyright protection. As soon as the work is completed, copyright is created. However, the work may be registered with the copyright office and such registration provides the best evidence in case of infringement. The copyright allows only the owner of the copyright to copy his work, perform, display, make derivative works, and to control sale and distribution of the work. Copyright law protects against copying of the work, but not if another person produces a very similar work independently. Courts nowadays infer from two criteria—whether the second person had access to the work of the first, and whether the work is truly similar or not. In case the two works are substantially similar and there was possible access to the original work, the court may conclude that there has been violation of copyright. In India, for most works, copyright is granted for a period of sixty years after the death of the author, however, in case the copyright is owned by an institution, it lasts sixty years from the date the work has been created.

Copyright law provides certain exceptions. The following are not necessarily copyright infringement. Some of these exceptions provided in the Indian Copyright Act are:

▶ Reproduction of judicial proceedings, court judgments, orders, etc.
▶ Reproduction of Acts of Legislature.

- ▶ Using copyright material for educational purposes—in class or examination.
- ▶ For research, criticism or review in newspapers, magazines, and other media.
- ▶ Reading or recitation in public.
- ▶ Playing music in certain clubs or performance to a non-paying audience or for religious institutions.
- ▶ Copies of computer programmes can be made or adapted for creating temporary or back-up copies.

Copyright can be transferred like any other property and an illuminating judgment from the Supreme Court of India drives the point home beautifully.

The Manipal Academy Case (Supreme Court of India, 2009)

Kota Shivarama Karanth was a *Jnanapeeth* awardee, who was a multi-faceted genius—a novelist, playwright, essayist, encyclopediationist, cultural anthropologist, artist, writer of science, environmentalist, etc. He was the Director of the Academy Of General Education, Manipal (the Manipal Academy) and had developed a new form of *Yakshagana* while he was working at the Manipal Academy: a new distinctive dance drama called 'Yaksha Ranga' which according to him meant 'Creative Extension of Traditional *Yakshagana*'. He had composed seven verses or *prasanga*s for staging *Yaksharanga* Ballet apart from bringing in changes to the traditional form, namely, *Raga, Tala*, scenic arrangement, costumes, etc. These *prasanga*s are: (i) *Bhishma Vijaya*; (ii) *Nala Damayanthi*; (iii) *Kanakangi or Kanakangi Kalyana*; (iv) *Abhimanyu or Abhimanyu Vadha*; (v) *Chitragadha or Babruvathana Kalaga*; (vi) *Panchavati*; and (vii) *Ganga Charitha*.

Malini Mallya had served Karanth in his old age with exemplary devotion and sincerity since 1974. Mallya also diligently cared for and nursed his wife, Leela Karanth, during her prolonged illness. In recognition of her devotion and sincere affection, he dedicated one of his novels namely, *'Antida Aparanji'* to her in 1986. He also placed on record her invaluable services to him in his memoirs, *'Hunchu Mansina Hathu Mukhagalu'* 1991 edition. Mallya had helped him write a bibliography of all his books after much research. She had also collected and edited all his stray writings from 1924 onwards in eight sumptuous volumes which were published by Mangalore University.

For all these services, Dr Karanth declared in his will that after his death, copyrights in respect of all his literary works shall belong to Mallya, and she alone would be entitled to receive royalties from all his books and she alone would be entitled to print, publish, and republish and market them. Whatever she might earn thereby shall be her exclusive income and property. No one else shall have any right or claim for the same.

It is in the light of these facts that we need to appreciate subsequent events. Karanth passed away in 1997. The above mentioned *Yakshagana* Ballet was performed in Delhi in September 2001 by the Manipal Academy. Mallya objected to such performance without her permission as she claimed that the copyright in the *Yakshagana* belonged to her and the Manipal Academy had no right to perform the dance drama without her permission. The Manipal Academy stated that Karanth had created the *Yakshagana* while he was working with the Academy and hence the Academy was the co-owner of the copyright and thus, there was no need for the Academy to ask her permission. She filed a case in the Udupi Court, which held in 2003 that she had the exclusive copyright in respect of the seven *prasanga*s which she acquired by reason of Karanth's will and the Manipal

Academy was restrained from performing the seven ballets or *prasanga*s or any parts thereof in any manner as evolved distinctively by Karanth.

The Manipal Academy filed an appeal before the Karnataka High Court. The appeal was dismissed. Thereafter, the Manipal Academy moved the Supreme Court for the same purpose. After deliberating on the matter in great detail and citing landmark cases like *RG Anand* versus *Delux Films* (1978) and *Eastern Book Company* versus *DB Modak* (2008), the court held that the copyright in respect of seven *prasanga*s and ballets vested with Mallya and, therefore, the Manipal Academy had infringed the copyright belonging to her. However, the court held that if the same performance had been made for educational purpose or before a non-paying audience or by an institution which comes within the purview of amateur club or society, it would not constitute any violation of copyright as such exceptions are provided under Section 52 of the Copyright Act.

This is a landmark judgment in India as it vindicates two well settled principles: (i) the copyright belongs to the author in the absence of a contract to the contrary between the author and the employer, (ii) intellectual property, namely copyright, can be transferred in a will as can any other property. It is important that the Supreme Court of India has recognized the importance of such copyright laws and has given due respect to the wishes of the author and owner of a copyrighted work. This judgment shall go a long way in creating a much better legal environment for protection of copyrighted works.

As copyright is for expression and not the idea, it creates a lot of problems and confusion, called the 'idea–expression dichotomy'. Of late, the controversy regarding the film '3 Idiots' and the claim made by Chetan Bhagat again brought to the fore the importance of the difference between idea and expression. A similar controversy had been the talk of the film industry in the 1950s regarding the filming of *New Delhi* in 1956. The matter finally was resolved in the Supreme Court about two decades later. Let us examine the case.

R.G. Anand v. *Delux Films* (Supreme Court of India, 1978)

R.G. Anand was an architect by profession and also a playwright, dramatist, and producer of stage plays. He had written and produced a number of plays like *Des Hamara*, *Azadi*, and *Election*. Thereafter, in 1953, he wrote a play, *Hum Hindustan*i, which was enacted for the first time in February 1954 in New Delhi under the auspices of the Indian National Theatre. The play proved to be very popular and received great approbation from the press and the public, as a result of which the play was restaged several times.

In November 1954, Anand received a letter from Mohan Sehgal, the proprietor of Delux Films, informing him that he had heard about the play *Hum Hindustani* by a common friend, Balwant Gargi, and would be interested to have a look at a copy of the play so that he may consider making a film based on it. Anand informed Sehgal that his play had been selected out of seventeen Hindi plays for the National Drama Festival which would be staged in December 1954, in Delhi. He invited him to see the play himself and examine the possibility of making the film. In January 1955, Sehgal met Anand in the latter's office in Delhi, where Anand read out and explained the entire play to him. He did not make any clear commitment but promised that he would inform Anand about his reaction after reaching Bombay. Anand did not hear anything from Sehgal. In May 1955, Sehgal announced the production of a film entitled, *New Delhi*. Anand came to know that this film was actually based on his play *Hum Hindustani* and wrote a letter expressing serious concern over the adaptation of his play into a film. Sehgal informed Anand that his doubts were without any foundation and assured him that the story treatment, dramatic construction, characters, etc., were quite different and bore not the remotest connection or resemblance with Anand's play.

New Delhi was released in September 1956. Anand saw the film and found that it was entirely based upon his play and was convinced that Sehgal, after having heard the play narrated to him, dishonestly imitated the same in his film and thus committed an act of piracy so as to result in violation of his copyright. He filed a suit for damages, accounts of the profits and permanent injunction against Sehgal.

Sehgal stated in the court that he had discussed with Balwant Gargi about making a new movie using 'provincialism' as its central theme. Hearing this, Gargi had asked Sehgal if he was interested in hearing the play *Hum Hindustani*, which was also based on provincialism. It was in this reference that a letter was written to Anand to provide a copy of the play. Sehgal admitted that Anand had read the play to him while he had visited Delhi and after hearing the play he had informed Anand that though the play might have been all right for the amateur stage, it was too inadequate for the purpose of making a full-length commercial motion picture. He denied that it was after hearing the play that he had decided to make the movie based on it. He further said that there could not be a copyright on the 'subject of provincialism' which can be used or adapted by anyone in his own way. He stated that *New Delhi* was quite different from the *Hum Hindustani* in content, spirit, and climax. There were surely some similarities between the film and the play, which could be explained by the fact that the idea of provincialism was the common source of the play and the film, for which Anand could not claim a copyright.

The trial judge decided that there was no violation of copyright by Sehgal. And though Anand filed an appeal in the Delhi High Court, it was also decided in favour of Sehgal. Later Anand appealed in the Supreme Court.

After going through the matter in great depth and explaining in detail nuances of copyright law, the Supreme Court held that the *idea* of provincialism cannot be protected by copyright. It held that on a close and careful comparison of the play and the film, but for the central idea (provincialism which is not protected by copyright), from scene to scene, situation to situation, in climax to anti-climax, pathos, bathos, in texture and treatment and purport and presentation, the film is materially different from the play.

The court also held that from a comparison of the scripts of *Hum Hindustani* and *New Delhi*, the authors of the film script have been influenced to a certain degree by the salient features of the plot set forth in the play. There can be little doubt from the evidence that the authors of the film script were aware of the scheme of the play. But on the other hand, the film travels beyond the plot delineated in the play.

This judgment, which is more than thirty years old—and pertains to a dispute of the 1950s—was and is still a landmark judgment in copyright law in India. This case brings out so clearly the distinction between *idea* and *expression*. The fundamental principle of copyright law is that idea cannot be protected. Only the expression of any such idea can be—and there may be a number of expressions for the same idea. In this case the filmmaker might have used the same idea and to a certain extent might have drawn inspiration from the plot, theme and characters of the play. However, the two expressions were so different that the court did not agree with the allegations of Anand that his play had been copied in a dishonest manner. This case highlights the importance of creativity and protection of creative ideas, which of course is extremely difficult and at times becomes a burden for the author. In most situations it would not be possible for the author to protect such ideas and the entire world is at liberty to 'copy' such an idea—or be inspired by that idea, a play with that idea, or work around the original expression in such a manner that the new expression appears to be entirely or substantially different from the first expression. We often see movies with similar ideas. A number have been made with the idea of 'rich boy, poor girl' or 'poor boy, rich girl'. Copyright law does not provide protection for such ideas.

PIRACY IN INDIA

India has most of the necessary intellectual property laws in place, yet enforcement of these laws is weak. There is rampant piracy of software, books, films, music, etc. There has been a trend in the last couple of years of a definite change in the mindset of foreign publishers, film studios and software companies, as the level of confidence and trust in the Indian legal enforcement machinery has gone up. The following troika of judgments bears testimony to this fact.

Harry Potter (Delhi High Court, 2010)

In 1996, JK Rowling entered into a publishing agreement with Bloomsbury Children's Books, a division of Bloomsbury Publishing, which is one of Europe's leading and most reputed independent publishing houses, especially in literary fiction, non-fiction and children books. She created the Harry Potter series in 1997, wrote the first book, *Harry Potter and the Philosopher's Stone* and since then, a number of Harry Potter books have been published. This series of children's books are a modern day publishing phenomenon and one of the most glaring success stories in the history of global publishing. In the last eight years more than 300 million copies of Harry Potter books have been sold worldwide in more than 200 countries and have been translated into sixty two languages—an unprecedented publishing achievement in a very short timespan.

In June 2000, Bloomsbury appointed Penguin Books India as its exclusive distributor in India for all their books published in the United Kingdom and the United States of America, including the Harry Potter series. In November 2006, Bloomsbury acquired all intellectual property rights, including copyrights of the artistic work comprising the cover of the UK edition of *Harry Potter and the Deathly Hallows*.

Rowling granted to Warner Bros. the rights to create motion pictures based on the Harry Potter books as well as the trademark rights and merchandising rights as regards the characters, titles, and other properties relating to the books. Warner Bros. also owns the copyrights and all other intellectual property rights in and of the visual reproduction of Harry Potter, including the logo of the Hogwarts School of Magic, all artwork and illustrations on the cover of the US editions of the series, including the recently released *Harry Potter and the Deathly Hallows*. Warner Bros. has applied for and obtained registration for the Harry Potter trademark, which includes all characters, book titles and films in India, under the provisions of the Trademark Act, 1999.

In July 2007, Bloomsbury was informed that police in Bangalore had seized 1500 copies of a book titled, *Harry Potter and the Deathly Hallows* from City Publication. The front cover of the seized books was identical to publication titled, *Harry Potter and the Deathly Hallows* and the back cover was identical to Warner Bros. artwork for it. These books were paperbacks and had been printed on very poor quality paper with cheap ink and seemed to be a pirated version of the original book.

A comparison of the infringing book with the original publication revealed the following:

a. The title of infringing book was identical to the title of Bloomsbury's publication *Harry Potter and the Deathly Hallows*.

b. The infringing book was falsely attributed to have been published by Bloomsbury and its name and mark appeared prominently on the front cover, spine, and title pages of the book.

c. The infringing book was falsely attributed to have been authored by Rowling and her name appeared prominently on the front and back cover, spine, and title pages of the book.

d. The copyright page in the infringing book had been reproduced verbatim without permission from Bloomsbury's preceding publication in the Harry Potter series namely *Harry Potter and the Half Blood Prince*.

e. The front cover of the infringing book was an unauthorized identical reproduction of the cover of the UK edition of Rowling's work titled *Harry Potter and the Deathly Hallows* published by Bloomsbury, wherein the copyright in art work comprising the cover vests with Bloomsbury.

f. The back cover of the infringing book was an unauthorized identical reproduction of the cover of the US edition of Rowling's work titled *Harry Potter and the Deathly Hallows* wherein the copyright in art work comprising the cover vests with Warner Bros.

g. The title page of the book contained an unauthorized reproduction of Warner Bros. artwork comprising the logo of the Hogwarts School of Magic. The aid logo of Hogwarts School appeared on the title page on all the publications in the Harry Potter series published by Bloomsbury.

h. A perusal of the contents of the book revealed that the same was an unauthorized adaptation of Rowling's works under the Harry Potter series as City Publication had without permission copied the characters, their names, the expression/description of the characters, their locations, actions, and accompaniments. Among other things, the following had been copied: the main character Harry Potter, the co-cast including Weasley, Hermione Granger, Professor Albus Dumbledore, the Dursleys including Uncle Vernon Dursley, Aunt Petunia Dursley, and Cousin Dudley Dursley, Lord Voldemort, amongst many others; the settings, locations for example the Dudley residence at Privet Drive, the Hogwarts Express—the train which took Harry Potter to the Hogwarts School of Magic, the Hogwarts School, etc.

This was done with mala fide intention to ride over the immense popularity of Rowling's works and the infringing book was deliberately printed and distributed within a week of the release of the original work. The genuine publication was much in demand all over India and the fake books were printed and distributed to mislead the public and fans of Harry Potter into buying the cheap imitation. Bloomsbury, Rowling and Warner Bros. filed a case against City Publication and demanded permanent injunction, rendition of accounts of profits, damages, delivery of fake books, etc. They alleged that such infringement had brought disrepute to them particularly to Rowling and is clearly a violation of copyright law. No one appeared on behalf of City Publication.

The court went into the matter and decided that by looking at the two works—the original and the infringing one—it was quite obvious that the infringing book was an unauthorized adaptation of the original book. The court held that it was a clear-cut case of copyright infringement including violation of Rowling's rights under copyright law in India. A permanent injunction was granted restraining the City Publication and others, their directors, partners, promoters, employees, officers, servants and agents including distributors, wholesalers and retailers, and all others acting for and on their behalf from printing, distributing, selling, offering for sale the infringing book *Harry Potter and the Deathly Hallows*. Thus, the court upheld Rowling's rights.

The court further ordered for permanent injunction, restraining City Publication, their directors, partners, promoters, employees, officers, servants, and agents including distributors, wholesalers, and retailers and all others acting for and on their behalf from using Warner Bros.' registered trademark Harry Potter and other associated trademarks on the cover, spine, title page of the infringing book and/or in the infringing book, or in any other manner amounting to infringement of Warner Bros.' registered trademarks. The court upheld the intellectual property rights of Warner Bros. which obtained the rights in an agreement with Rowling.

The court also ordered for delivery to Rowling, Bloomsbury and Warner Bros. all the duplicating equipment and other infringing material.

This is a very important decision where foreign publishers and writers have taken infringement and piracy very seriously and taken legal recourse to create deterrence for such unscrupulous publishers and sellers who blatantly violate copyright law. Such a judgment shall go a long way in sending the right message that the judiciary in India will not allow rampant infringement. This judgment will surely help in creating a desirable legal environment for protection of intellectual property, particularly copyright in India.

Adobe and Microsoft (Delhi High Court, 2009)

Adobe Systems and Microsoft Corporation, both American companies, develop and market software programmes which are also included in the definition of a 'literary work' under the Copyright Act, 1957 in India. These are also protected in India under the International Copyright Order, 1999. India protects the rights of authors and member countries of the Berne and Universal Copyright Conventions. Both India and the USA are signatories to the Universal Copyright Convention as well as the Berne Convention.

Adobe and Microsoft came to know that a company providing consultancy services to call centre start-ups was extensively using pirated software programmes for its computer system at the office for day-to-day business activities. This was reported by BSA/NASSCOM (BSA—Business Software Alliance, NASSCOM—National Association of Software and Services Companies) anti-piracy hotline.

Adobe and Microsoft filed the case in the Delhi High Court and were granted an ex parte injunction restraining the company and its representatives, agents and all other persons acting for and on its behalf from using the pirated and unlicenced software. The court also appointed an Advocate Commissioner to visit the premises and find out the details of the infringing software, who reported the presence of counterfeit and unlicenced software in a number of computer disks. The company never appeared in court.

Adobe and Microsoft filed an affidavit giving details of blatant violation of their copyrights and end-user piracy which was going on in a deliberate manner. The potential revenue loss was estimated approximately Rs 16 lakhs as per the following details:

Name of software	Approx. Cost of licenced software	No. of Computers having pirated versions	Approx. revenue loss
Microsoft Windows 98 (Standard)	Rs 6000/- per licence	15	Rs 90,000
Microsoft Windows Office (Standard)	Rs15000/- per unit	21	Rs 3,15,000
Microsoft Server SQL 7.0	Rs 35,000/- per unit	2	Rs 70,000
Microsoft Project (various versions)	Rs16,000/- per unit	4	Rs 64,000
Microsoft Windows 2000 Server	Rs 27,000/- per unit	5	Rs1,35,000/-
Microsoft Visio 2000	Rs 20,000/- per unit	1	Rs 20,000/-
Microsoft Windows 2000 PRO	Rs 7,000/- per unit	3	Rs 21,000/-

Microsoft Exchange Server (various versions)	Rs 36,000/- per unit	1	Rs 36,000/-
Microsoft Visual Studio 6.0	Rs 50,000/- per unit	3	Rs 1,50,000/-
Microsoft Windows NT 4.0 Server	Rs 36,000/- per unit	1	Rs 36,000/-
Adobe Acrobat (various versions)	Rs 15,000/- per unit	3	Rs 45,000/-
Adobe Page Maker (various versions)	Rs 25,000/- per unit	3	Rs 75,000/-
Adobe Photoshop (various versions)	Rs 25,000/- per unit	6	Rs 1,50,000/-
Macromedia Dreamweaver	Rs 50,000/- per unit	3	Rs 1,50,000/-
Macromedia Fireworks 3.0	Rs 60,000/- per unit	2	Rs 1,20,000/-
Macromedia Flash	Rs 50,000/- per unit	2	Rs 1,00,000/-
Total			Rs 15,77,000/-

After going through the matter, the Delhi High Court decided that there was undisputed infringement of statutory rights of Adobe and Microsoft in respect of the software for which copyright exists. The use of counterfeit and duplicate software was clearly illegal which cost financial damage and loss of reputation. Such practice should never be permitted in a country which aims to provide better intellectual property protection and thus the court granted permanent injunction to Adobe and Microsoft. The court granted Rs 5 lakhs by way of compensatory damages, as well as Rs 5 lakhs on account of punitive damages and held that the award of punitive damages was aimed at deterring a wrongdoer and the like minded from indulging in such unlawful activities.

This is a very interesting case where big multinational corporations like Adobe and Microsoft made a joint effort to file a matter in a legal forum in India, giving the signal to businessmen in India and abroad that they will protect their intellectual property rights by using all available legal means and shall not shy away from going to court against piracy. The case also highlights a perceptible change in the attitude of the judiciary, as awards of punitive damages are rare in India. This gives a clear message that Indian courts are now willing to protect the rights of lawful owners of intellectual property by applying the black letter law in a much more liberal and effective manner.

Warner Bros. v. *Cinema Paradiso* (Delhi High Court, 2009)

Warner Bros., along with its associated and affiliated companies are the owners, co-owners, assignees, licensees of rights and titles, and have interests in the copyrights of films produced by them.

'Cinema Paradiso' rents out DVDs in Hyderabad and some other cities. It has two categories of members—individual and corporate. It charges a refundable 'caution deposit of Rs 2000' and a 'processing' and 'application fee'. Thereafter a rental fee of Rs 75, and in some cases Rs 100, is charged against each title rented. The rental DVDs can be collected by customers from the shop or delivered to them. Several DVDs so hired out, bear the warning that such DVDs are not permitted for sale or rental outside the US and Canada.

Cinema Paradiso developed a website (www.cinema paradiso shop.com) where it claimed to be making available all the DVDs under a licence. The website stated:

First DVD store with all licence

Though DVDs are easily available, piracy is rampant, Cinema Paradiso is an exception. Great caution has been exercised to ensure that only original DVDs are stocked. In fact, Cinema Paradiso is the first DVD store in India to obtain complete license for its functioning. Further, it is the only store to have obtained legal consultations and the assent of the registered organization against film piracy. What's more, each DVD in the store is copyrighted to avoid any issues pertaining to piracy.

Contrary to claims, Cinema Paradiso was making available for rental purposes films in which Warner Bros. had copyright protection without any authority or licence from them. Warner Bros. decided to take legal action.

A little bit of background about releasing of films in theatres, home video, etc. will be helpful in appreciating the matter.

As film production is a complex, time consuming, and costly process, it needs a well-defined distribution strategy for its commercial success. Films are generally released in different stages—in theatres, later as home video, rental, cable, and satellite TV. The time difference between the release in theaters and release on other formats may be a few months, or at times, a couple of years. This distribution strategy and system of release is commonly referred to as 'windows'. In the first stage it is vital that the film is available to the public only at theaters. In the second window the film is normally released as a home video. Thereafter, the film is set for release through other windows and media. It is critical to protect the film from being distributed on any media other than that selected by the copyright owner. In case it is not followed strictly, the strategy is likely to fail and the copyright owner may not be able to commercially exploit the film fully.

Films are also distributed and made available to the public in different formats at different times. Warner Bros. first releases its films in theaters in the US. By the time the film is released in theaters in other countries, the film may already be released in home video format in the US. Thus it is possible that at a time when a film is released in theaters in India, the same film might have been released on home video format in the US. It is thus important and essential that the home video released in the US is not authorized for sale or rental outside the US. The DVDs are coded according to specific geographical zones—for sale in the US as zone 1 and for sale in India as zone 5. DVDs coded for zone 1 are not authorized to be sold or rented in any other zone.

Warner Bros. alleged that there was a deep-rooted nexus between Cinema Paradiso and cable operators. The DVDs were imported from the US and rented out in India and the cable operators were using the imported DVDs for telecast on the cable network. Even a single film rental is capable of causing irreparable injury and damage to Warner Bros. When telecast by cable operators, the film reaches several million homes all over India. By that time, the film might have been released in India only in theatres as the first window. In such instances, the damage surely would be immeasurable and irreparable. Warner Bros. alleged that in the absence of any licence with Cinema Paradiso, its conduct was indisputably an act of infringement of copyright.

Cinema Paradiso defended itself by the following arguments: that there was no infringement of copyright as it had purchased the DVDs from authorized sources outside India. Further, by applying the principles of the doctrine of exhaustion of rights, the copyright of Warner Bros. exhausts when a copy of the film has been sold from authorized sources to a purchaser. It was thus free to rent out such DVDs in India.

DOCTRINE OF EXHAUSTION

The doctrine of exhaustion of copyright enables free trade in material objects on which copies of protected works have been fixed and put into circulation with the right holder's consent. The 'exhaustion' principle in a sense arbitrates the conflict between the right to own a copy of a work and the author's right to control the distribution of copies. Exhaustion is decisive with respect to the priority of ownership and the freedom to trade in material carriers on the condition that a copy has been legally brought into trading. Transfer of ownership of a carrier with a copy of a work fixed on it makes it impossible for the owner to derive further benefits from the exploitation of a copy that was traded with his consent. The exhaustion principle is thus termed legitimate by reason of the profits earned for the ownership transfer, which should be satisfactory to the author if the work is not being exploited in a different exploitation field.

Cinema Paradiso also stated that zoning is a matter of convenience in terms of technology and not a copyright notice and at best zoning is a way of asserting market dominance rather than enforcing an intellectual property right. It also argued that according to the Constitution of India, freedom of speech and expression is a fundamental right and providing entertainment is an integral part of such a fundamental right. Thus, it was seeking to exercise its fundamental right. Moreover, it was operating in the nature of a film club rather than a pure rental business.

The court discussed the matter in great detail and concluded that Cinema Paradiso was infringing Warner Bros. copyright, and cannot rent films without a licence from Warner Bros. The court held that exhaustion of rights is linked to distribution rights and the exhaustion principle cannot be inferred automatically. The court gave an analogy to reject the stand taken by Cinema Paradiso that the moment a licencee or a customer gets a copy of the copyrighted work, copyright owners would exhaust their rights, enabling the licencees to exploit the copies uninhibitedly.

The Analogy

If a distributor is given a copy to exhibit a film in territory A, or hire them in that territory; he could, by extension of Cinema Paradiso's logic, travel beyond that territory, or use a rental copy to exhibit the film in another territory where it has not been released or even rent it in such territory, and so on. To give another instance—the purchase of a rental copy meant to be used in the southern region, in India, designated by the copyright owner, analogically, can, according to Cinema Paradiso, be rented out in other regions too, whether or not such films are released in those regions. Such renting out may have catastrophic commercial consequences: one of the buyers/renters might well be a cinema theatre, which may exhibit the film in public. This would completely defeat the copyright owner's right to commercially exploit the film, and for that purpose, partition the market at its convenience. The safeguard provided by Section 51 (b) (iv) proviso, in the case of importation of one infringing copy, amply testifies that if importation is for private use of the importer, which specifically alludes to the non-commercial use by such a person or individual, it is not deemed an infringement.

The court also rejected Cinema Paradiso's contention that allowing such business was in the public interest and a fundamental right as guaranteed by the Constitution of India. The court said that if such films are not available in India, Cinema Paradiso and any other interested person is always free to negotiate the terms of a licence with Warner Bros. and other film companies.

This is a very important and interesting judgment, because it is common knowledge that sale of pirated DVDs is widespread in India. Unfortunately, little or no action is taken against such sellers. When such an illegal business is being conducted in a fairly organized manner, as was the case with Cinema Paradiso, the copyright owners shall have recourse to courts in India and with the changing mood, courts shall not allow such shameless and obvious copyright violation. The message is clear that copyright protection for films and music will become stronger in the near future. Also, fundamental rights can never be interpreted to allow someone to commit a theft—whether of physical or intellectual property.

TECHNOLOGY

With the rapid growth in technology, particularly computers and the Internet, it has become very easy to make copies of many things. It can literally be done with the click of a button. New challenges have come up in the form of file sharing, downloading, etc. Let us examine a very interesting case involving 'Grokster' which shares a suffix with the infamous 'Napster'.

MGM v. Grokster (US Supreme Court, 2005)

Grokster distributed free software that allowed computer users to share electronic files through peer-to-peer networks. These computers communicated directly with each other and not through central servers. Billions of files were shared across such networks each month and most of these shared files were copyrighted music and video files, sent without authorization. Interestingly, Grokster promoted its software to infringe copyright and presented it as an alternative to the notorious file sharing service, Napster, which was sued by copyright holders for facilitating copyright infringement. Grokster did not receive any revenue from users but generated income by selling advertising space. As the number of users increased, so did advertising opportunities. Grokster made no effort to filter copyright material from users' downloads.

MGM studios (Metro-Goldwyn-Mayer), copyright holders of a number of films and other works, filed a case against Grokster and the matter finally reached the US Supreme Court. The court decided that Grokster was clearly liable for infringement of copyright and gave the following reasons:

First, Grokster targeted the market comprising the earlier Napster users. Second, it never attempted to develop filtering tools or other mechanisms to diminish the infringing activity using its software and third, it made money by selling advertising space. The court held that there was an intent to bring about infringement and distribute a device suitable for infringing use. The court also observed that there was a tension between the competing values of supporting creativity through copyright protection and promoting technological innovation by limiting infringement liability.

The court also referred to an earlier case—the Sony VCR—which was based on the concept of 'time-shifting', that is, recording a programme for later viewing at a more convenient time. Universal Studios had taken Sony to court. In that case the US Supreme Court had held that there was no evidence that Sony had desired to bring about taping in violation of copyright or that they had taken active steps to increase its profits from unlawful taping. Sony was not held liable because the VCR was 'capable of commercially significant non-infringing uses'.

Similarly, in a recent case in June 2010, the United States District Court for the Southern District of New York rejected Viacom's claim that YouTube was guilty of massive copyright infringement. The court held that YouTube fully qualifies for 'safe harbour' protections under the American Digital Millennium Copyright Act (DMCA). It is said that Viacom and other copyright owners are responsible to police and monitor YouTube to prevent infringement. Once YouTube receives any such information, it is legally under an obligation to implement compliant notices and take-down procedures as laid down by the DMCA. YouTube has been doing this as per the law. Viacom has decided to appeal in the US Court of Appeals for the Second Circuit.

PLAGIARISM

In a lighter vain it is said that, 'if you copy from one source, it is plagiarism; and if you copy from several sources, it is research'. However, plagiarism is a very serious issue and goes to the root of copying someone's expression or an idea in such a manner that it becomes quite obvious that it has been copied. It can be a close imitation. Almost all the acts of copyright infringement shall amount to plagiarism but it is not true the other way round. For instance, copying from a work for which copyright has expired without giving due credit to the author shall amount to plagiarism.

There have been so many incidents of plagiarism, however, two of them from the recent past are as follows:

Mashelkar Committee Report

A committee was constituted by the Government of India in April 2005 to review patent law, headed by RA Mashelkar. In December 2006, the committee submitted its report. The conclusion contained about nine to ten sentences that were taken verbatim from Shamnad Basheer's paper on *Limiting the Patentability of Pharmaceutical Inventions and Micro-organisms*. The report was withdrawn on the grounds of 'technical inaccuracy and plagiarism'.

Kaavya Viswanathan

In 2006, Kaavya Viswanathan, a Harvard student accepted that she had borrowed the language from Megan F McCafferty's novels *Sloppy Firsts* and *Second Helpings* in her novel, *How Opal Mehta Got Kissed, Got Wild and Got a Life*. Kaavya later made a formal apology.

Such incidents have neither been the first nor the last.

MUSIC—INSPIRATION OR COPYING

Music directors in India have long been inspired by Western music and have used very popular Western numbers in Bollywood films. Whether this is a violation of copyright or not remains a moot question as both the Western and its inspired number in India became highly popular and over the years gained a lot of respect. There are dozens and dozens of such songs. Some of these are:

▶ The song *'Zindagi mil ke bitayenge'* in the movie *Satte pe Satta*, which was inspired from the 1954 movie *Seven Brides for Seven Brothers* was inspired by *'The Longest Day March'* (1962).

- The number '500 miles' (*If you miss the train I'm on...*) inspired the song *'Jab koi baat bigad jaye'* in the film *Jurm*.
- Stevie Wonder's *'I just called to say I love you'* inspired the title song *'Aate jaate, hanste gaate'* in the film *Maine Pyaar Kiya*.
- Shammi Kapoor's movie *Dil de ke dekho* (1959) had the title song inspired by 1953 McGuire Sisters' *'Sugartime'*. Usha Khanna was the music director.
- R.D. Burman was inspired by Donavan's *'If it's Tuesday, this must be Belgium'* while composing the music for *'Chura liya hai tum ne jo dil ko'* in the film *Yaadon ki Baraat*.
- R.D. Burman borrowed heavily from Demis Roussos's *'Say you love me'* for the highly successful and popular *Sholay* number *'Mehbooba mehbooba'*.
- Anu Malik was truly inspired by Nusrat Fateh Ali Khan's *'Mera piya ghar aya O Lalni'* while composing the music for Madhuri Dixit's popular number *'Mera piya ghar aya O Ramji'* in the 1995 film *Yaraana*, which was inspired by the American movie *Sleeping with the Enemy* featuring Julia Roberts.

FOOD FOR THOUGHT

The Rural Telephone Service Company is a certified public utility providing telephone service to several communities in Kansas. It publishes a typical telephone directory, consisting of white pages and yellow pages. It obtains data for the directory from subscribers, who must provide their names and addresses to obtain telephone service. Feist Publications is a publishing company that specializes in area-wide telephone directories, covering a much larger geographic range. When Rural refused to licence its white pages listings to Feist, it extracted the listings from Rural's directory without Rural's consent. Although Feist altered many of Rural's listings, several were identical to listings in Rural's white pages. Rural filed a copyright infringement suit. Decide?

FILL IN THE BLANKS

i) Copyright registration provides the best _____ in case of infringement cases.

ii) The copyright expires _____ years after the death of the author of a book.

iii) Grokster followed in the footsteps of _____.

TRUE OR FALSE

a) Copyright protection is granted to an idea.

b) It is essential to register for copyright to get any protection under the copyright law.

c) Though copyright law is strict in India, its enforcement leaves much to be desired.

d) India does not provide copyright protection to foreign works.

KEY TO FILL IN THE BLANKS

i)   Evidence
ii) Sixty
iii) Napster

TRUE FALSE

a)   False
b)   False
c)   True
d)   False

4

Trademarks

Have you ever visited a 'Bala' shoe store? There are a number of such stores in India that write Bala in cursive style so that it may appear as Bata, the famous, trusted footwear brand. Similarly, there are a good number of products—face cream, talcum powder, etc.—sold as 'Pond' or 'Ponds' to associate the product with the well established and famous Pond's brand. These instances and several like them are infringement of registered trademarks, where imitators purposefully try to confuse the public, which is punishable by law. Let us discuss the salient features of trademarks.

SALIENT FEATURES

Trademark protection is a statutory protection which extends to a mark capable of being represented graphically and capable of distinguishing the goods or services of one entity from those of others. This may include shape, packaging and colour combinations. This mark may be a logo, symbol, brand, heading, label, ticket, name, signature, word, letter etc. With the 1999 Trademark Law enacted in India, services have also been included under the ambit of trademarks. These services include banking, communication, education, financing, insurance, real estate, transport, storage, energy supply, boarding, lodging, entertainment, etc.

The law also defines a well-known trademark as a mark which may be used for particular goods or services. Problems arise when a trademark, which is known to the public to such a degree that use of such a mark in relation to other goods or services would likely cause confusion in the minds of the public. An interesting case on the point is the Benz versus VIP undergarments case, which we shall discuss later in the chapter.

Trademarks are registered for a period of ten years, and can be renewed periodically which makes it almost perpetual. Thus, if proper care is taken to renew and maintain them, trademarks are like diamonds, they last forever. These characteristics of trademarks make them one of the most important intellectual property assets for companies owning famous brands and also for companies aspiring to make their trademarks popular and well-known.

The scope of a trademark is growing larger and now includes shape, colour, sound, fragrance, slogans, motion marks, temporary marks, etc. Today, businesses want protection for almost everything related to their products in the form of trademarks for the simple reason that trademarks are perpetual.

There is also a concept of trade dress which is a much broader concept than trademark. For example, colour combinations used in a restaurant, seating arrangements, selection of furniture and overall ambience and feel can be protected under trade dress. This type of protection is not common in India. Regarding trade dress, we shall discuss the Taco Cabana case as contradistinguished with the ITC Bukhara case.

India's legal system is based on the common law system—law as determined by judges. In this system, even an unregistered trademark recieves legal protection under the law of 'passing off'. That is, the imitator is trying to 'pass off' his goods as original goods by copying the mark and trying to confuse customers. Though such protection is provided by law, it is advisable that a company register its trademarks. The company should also make it known to the public at large that it is serious about protecting its trademarks. This can be done by making press releases, cautionary notices and advertising the mark. It is also imperative to register and protect the domain name and be vigilant when any copying is found to be taking place. Satyam Infoway a company that later gained infamy due to the Satyam scam, is an interesting case; one we shall discuss later in the chapter. The owner of a trademark must necessarily take urgent steps against the infringer. Infringement of a trademark can be either by using an identical mark or using a deceptively or confusingly similar mark. Once the trademark is registered the owner can use the symbol $^®$. However the symbol 'TM' can be used even without registration and it implies that one claims to own the trademark.

The law regarding trademarks in India is the Trade Marks Act, 1999. Prior to this the law was the Trade and Merchandise Marks Act, 1958. The new law complies with TRIPS requirements and provides better and stronger protection to trademarks including service marks, collective marks and certification marks. A collective mark is used for several goods which come from a particular group or organization. For instance, 'Brooke Bond' is used as a Collective Mark for its brands—Red Label, Taj Mahal, and Taaza.

A certification mark certifies that a product meets with certain standards associated with that mark. For instance, 'Woolmark' certifies that goods are made of 100 percent wool or the mark 'ISI' by Bureau of Indian Standards.

A soundmark is an unconventional trademark, and though it has been granted for several decades in the US, it was granted for the first time in India recently to Yahoo's yodel. American examples include the soundtrack of MGM's lion roar, the distinctive introduction music of 20th Century Fox, and the NBC chimes: the boradcaster's tonal ID became the first in the US to be accepted as an 'audio or sound mark' in 1950.

Colour trademarks can also be registered for single, multiple, or combinations of colours (Coke's red and white, for example). The US Supreme Court held in the Qualitex case that even a single colour may be protected under trademark law. We shall review this case later in the chapter. Other examples are Cadbury's purple and Tiffany's blue.

Shapes can also be protected as a trademark. Coke's contour bottle is one of the few packages to receive a trademark. The shape of the bottle creates a unique visual identity and distinguishes Coca Cola from all other products. It is however quite difficult to get a trademark just for the shape. The new Indian law provides such protection.

Smells and fragrances can also be protected as trademarks if they are so unique that a product can be associated with that smell and customers can distinguish the product, however, the smell should not serve any functional purpose. These marks are highly contentious, as by definition fragrance of perfumes cannot be trademarked as they are functional—the purpose of a perfume is to provide fragrance. However, certain courts have allowed such protection. Thus, it is not a settled issue, and it is surely extremely difficult to be granted smell mark protection. An example is Sumitomo Rubber, who trademarked a floral fragrance reminiscent of roses as applied to tyres. This may sound strange. You'd think customers would depend more on the logo and name of the manufacturing company rather than a tyre's smell while purchasing it, but there you are. Until now, no smell mark has been registered in India.

There have been very interesting and illuminating judgments

from different courts in India and abroad. I have chosen a couple of them which illustrate various aspects of trademarks. The first one is one of the most famous judgments about trademarks in India—the Whirlpool case.

Whirlpool (Supreme Court of India, 1996)

Whirlpool USA is a multinational company and a worldwide market leader in washing machines. In 1956-57, it obtained registration for the trademark 'Whirlpool' in India in respect of clothes dryers, washers, dishwashers and some other electrical appliances. These registrations were renewed periodically. In 1977, Whirlpool USA did not apply for renewal and thus the registration lapsed in India. In 1987, Whirlpool USA formed a joint venture with TVS and filed an application with the Registrar of Trademarks for registration of trademark 'Whirlpool' for certain goods including washing machines. Prior to this, in 1986, Usha–Shriram had filed to trademark 'Whirlpool', which was advertised in the trademark journal in 1988. Whirlpool USA opposed it in 1989, which was dismissed in 1992 and Usha-Shriram was allowed registration of the trademark 'Whirlpool' and this registration was granted from 1987, the date of the application.

Whirlpool's Contention
Whirlpool USA filed a case in the Delhi High Court and later in the Supreme Court of India. It claimed to have a worldwide trade and non-renewal of its trademark in India due to the then imports restrictions and foreign trade policy of the Government of India. (Remember the time when Coke and IBM were kicked out of the country). The production of the goods (washing machines) never stopped and these were marketed and exported to India without renewal of registration of trademark. They were continuously

advertised and there was no 'abandonment' of the trademark. It really cared for its rights and hence started legal proceedings the moment it came to know that the trademark has been adopted by Usha-Shriram.

Usha–Shriram's Defence

Usha-Shriram submitted that because the trademark 'Whirlpool' was abandoned by the American company, it had the right to use it. There was no question of passing-off as it was manufacturing and selling washing machines at less than 1/3rd the price of American washing machines and a full description was given on the plate affixed to the washing machines, leaving no room for any confusion in the minds of the buyer.

The court, after going through the pleadings and hearing arguments of lawyers of both parties, held that Whirlpool USA had acquired a trans-border reputation and there was no plausible explanation offered by Usha-Shriram for adopting the mark 'Whirlpool' when it was selling its products in the name of Usha-Shriram, Usha-Lexus, etc. The only inference which can be derived was that Usha-Shriram sought the unfair advantage of using the 'Whirlpool' trademark and ride on the global reputation of the American company. The Indian courts could not allow conduct that would cause irreparable injury to the American company's reputation and goodwill.

This is a landmark judgment where the American company did not renew the trademark, however regained the protection from law on the basis of its global reputation, spill-over effect of its reputation, goodwill, and trans-border reputation; giving it the status of a well-known trademark. In ordinary circumstances, the courts might have gone ahead with the literal interpretation, which clearly states that if a mark has not been renewed, protection cannot be granted to such a mark. It is analogous to the situation when someone's driving licence has expired, they are forbidden by law to drive on the road, even though he might be the world's best driver. However, the Supreme Court in this case went ahead with the global trend of providing better and stronger protection to trademarks and allowed Whirlpool USA's case. This case gave the right signal to foreign companies desirous of doing business in India and it was a decision made in line with India's economic liberalization policies of the early 1990s.

Another interesting case is Mercedes Benz, the name of the German carmaker being used to sell undergarments.

Benz v. *VIP Undergarments* (Delhi High Court, 1993)

Mercedes Benz is a vehicle brand known all over the world and is recognized by its symbol, a three-pointed star in a circle. This German brand is so well-known and so expensive that the name and the mark are synonymous with luxury and good taste. Benz is known to almost anyone who has ever used a quality car or aspires to use a luxury car. The name Benz as applied to a car has a unique place in the world. Long ago, Mercedes Benz collaborated with the Tatas in India to produce Mercedes Benz–Tata Trucks which were used in India in very large numbers. Thus it would be unbelievable if any person in India says they have not heard about Benz.

VIP undergarments began selling an underwear with the name 'VIP-Benz' and advertised it with the photograph of a man wearing the same underwear with his legs separated and hands joined together above his shoulders, and the sun rays producing a halo effect to form a circle around the joined hands and the separated legs, thus forming the three pointed star of Benz in a circle. The advertisement also came with the following description:

'German Perfection. It need not be restricted to mere machines.'

Towards the bottom, it mentioned:

New VIP Benz steers a touch of German precision to men's underwear. You have the most comfortable stretchable fabric. And you have the most reliable imported rubber elastic. The rest is sheer style. All perfect. All German.

The boxes also used the same photograph of the man with his legs separated and hands joined within a circle. Thus, it indicated a strong link between the three-pointed star of Mercedes Benz and undergarments sold by VIP.

Mercedes Benz Contention

Mercedes Benz asked VIP to refrain from selling the undergarments with the name Benz, to which VIP paid no attention. Later Benz filed a case in the Delhi High Court on the grounds that the 'Benz' mark is well-known globally and should not be used for any other product without its permission. As Benz is the trade name for a very high priced and extremely well engineered car, VIP should be ordered not to dilute that brand name by using it in connection to a product like underwear.

VIP's Defence

VIP defended itself by saying that Benz has not registered itself for undergarments in India and, moreover, the undergarment name was based on the name of the city Mercedes, which is a city in South America. The court however, was not convinced with this argument as it held that most people have not heard about this city. The judge categorically stated that neither he nor the counsel for VIP had heard about this city prior to this case. The court held that there was no reason why any trader in India should adopt the name Benz which is associated with one of the finest cars in the world and use the same name with respect to undergarments. The court did not even agree to VIP's counsel's request to allow selling the existing stock. The court remarked that destruction or non-use of such goods would send a clear message to businessmen that they should not try to demean other people's name and reputation by using a name like Benz for their goods. VIP was ordered not to use the name Benz and the three-pointed human being in a ring.

This case is one of those first judgments in which the court demonstrated the change in the attitude of the judiciary post-liberalization and globalization. It was a clear message that the courts would not allow the use of well-known trademarks like Benz for products with whom they have no connection whatsoever. This case was a landmark judgment and gave the desired level of confidence to foreign companies that their marks would have proper legal protection in India and that the legal environment in India was changing for the better.

In another instance, Amul, famous for dairy products, tried to use the expression 'Sugar Free' and got into trouble with Cadila's 'Sugar Free'.

Cadila v. Amul (Delhi High Court, 2007)

Cadila is one of the largest pharmaceutical companies in India and has used the trademark 'Sugar Free' since 1988. Later, the trademark 'Sugar Free' was used as an umbrella trademark in relation to its various products, namely, 'Sugar Free Natura', 'Sugar Free Gold' and 'Sugar Free D'lite'. Cadila had incurred huge expenses in promoting and popularizing its products under the trademark, both via electronic and print media. Cadila stated that due to excellent quality and a high degree of efficiency, the Sugar

Free range of products enjoy immense goodwill and reputation among medical professionals, traders and the public.

The Gujarat Co-operative Milk Marketing Federation Limited, makers of the well-known dairy products 'Amul' began using the expression 'Sugar Free' on its 'Pro Biotic Frozen Dessert'. The expression 'Amul-Sugar Free Pro Biotic Frozen Dessert' has been printed on the packages. It somehow gives an impression that it is connected more to 'Sugar Free' rather than Amul. Unusually large font size has been adopted for the expression 'Sugar Free' and Amul has been written in a smaller font size. Thus the words Sugar Free are much more conspicuous than the trademark Amul. The entire packaging is such that the focus is on the word Sugar Free and Amul is completely overshadowed.

Cadila filed the case in the Delhi High Court and asked the court to order Amul not to use the words Sugar Free, which is Cadila's registered trademark.

Amul defended itself by stating that 'Sugar Free' was a commonly used, essentially descriptive expression. Thus, Cadila cannot have an exclusive right to use the words Sugar Free. Any other manufacturer making confectionery, biscuits, dairy products, desserts, etc. which do not contain any sugar, should be able to use 'Sugar Free' to convey the message that the product is without sugar. Cadila objected and stated that there are other methods which can be used to convey the meaning, for example, no sugar, without sugar, free of sugar, etc. The court however, did not agree with Cadila's argument that by trademarking Sugar Free, no other manufacturer can use the expression to convey the meaning that its products are without sugar. The court also held that the fact that the trademark has acquired a secondary meaning and is distinctive by itself is not conclusive. To establish a case that one product has been passed off as another successfully, Cadila had to establish before the court that Amul misrepresented its products as that of Cadila's and thus caused damage to the distinctiveness associated with the trademark. The court said that no such case has been made by Cadila.

The court was however convinced that there was a definite possibility of confusion in the present case due to the much larger font size of Sugar Free as compared to the smaller font size of Amul on the packages of frozen desserts, and Amul should not be allowed to use the expression 'Sugar Free' in the present font size. 'Sugar Free' should not be bigger than its trademark. The court allowed Amul to use the expression Sugar Free as part of a sentence or as a catchy legend so as to describe the characteristic feature of its product.

This is a case where a commonly used expression like 'Sugar Free' was a given a trademark and in hindsight it appears that such a trademark, which is purely descriptive in nature, should never have been granted to Cadila. The best trademarks are supposed to be those which do not describe the product and have been coined by the manufacturer, which in fact convey no meaning or are absolutely unrelated to the product, for example, Apple for computers, Diesel and Mango for luxury clothing, etc.

Domain names are very valuable intellectual property for companies and the following case illustrates it wonderfully.

Satyam Infoway v. *Siffynet Solutions* (Supreme Court of India, 2004)

Satyam Infoway Limited was incorporated in 1995 and registered several domain names like www.sify.net, www.sifymall.com, www.sifyrealestate.com, etc. in June 1999 with the internationally recognized Registrars, the Internet Corporation for Assigned Names and Numbers (ICANN) and the World Intellectual Property

Organization (WIPO). The word 'Sify' is a coined word which Satyam invented by using elements of its corporate name, Satyam Infoway. It attained a wide reputation with the name. That was surely much before the Satyam scam and revelation made by Ramalinga Raju.

Siffynet Solutions began Internet marketing under the domain names of www.siffynet.net and www.siffynet.com from June 5, 2001. The difference is of one extra 'f'. It obtained registration of its two domain names with ICANN.

Satyam came to know that Siffynet was using the word 'Siffy' as part of its domain name and served a notice to cease and desist from carrying on business in the name of Siffynet and to transfer the domain names to Satyam. Siffynet refused to do so. Left with no option, Satyam filed a suit in the Civil Court on the basis that Siffynet was passing off its business and services as someone else's by using Satyam's business and domain name. The Court granted temporary injunction. Siffynet preferred an appeal before the High Court which granted an interim stay on the Civil Judge's judgment. Satyam challenged this order in the Supreme Court. It is clear that both the Civil and the High Court proceeded on the basis that the principles relating to passing off actions in connection with trademarks are applicable to domain names.

Siffynet's Arguments

Siffynet contended that a domain name could not be confused with 'property names' such as trademarks, and that a domain name is merely an address on the Internet. Registration of a domain name with ICANN did not confer any intellectual property right; and it is a contract with a registration authority allowing communication to reach the owner's computer via Internet links channelled through the registration authority's server and that it is akin to registration of a company name which is a unique identifier of a company but of itself confers no intellectual property rights.

Supreme Court's Observations about Domain Names

The Supreme Court observed that the original role of a domain name was no doubt to provide an address for computers on the Internet. But the Internet has developed from a mere means of communication to a mode of carrying on commercial activity. With the increase of commercial activity on the Internet, a domain name is also used as a business identifier. Therefore, the domain name not only serves as an address for Internet communication but also identifies the specific Internet site. In the commercial field, each domain name owner provides information/services, which are associated with their domain name. Thus, a domain name may pertain to provision of services within the meaning of the Trademarks Act, 1999. A domain name is easy to remember and use, and is chosen as an instrument of commercial enterprise not only because it facilitates the ability of consumers to navigate the Internet to find websites they are looking for, but also at the same time, serves to identify and distinguish the business itself, or its goods or services, and to specify its corresponding online Internet location.

Passing Off

An action for passing off, as the phrase 'passing off' itself suggests, is to restrain the competitor/imitator from passing off its goods or services to the public as that of a pre-existing manufacturer or service provider. It is an action not only to preserve the reputation of the latter but also to safeguard the public. The second important element in a passing off action is misrepresentation—which may be intentional or innocent. The real test is establishing the likelihood of confusion in the minds of actual or potential customers or users. These customers are not expected to have an extraordinary memory. Thus the test is 'imperfect recollection of a person of ordinary memory'. The third essential element of a passing off action is loss or the likelihood of it.

The use of the same or similar domain name may lead to a diversion of users which could result from such users mistakenly accessing one domain name instead of another. This may occur in e-commerce with its rapid progress and instant and almost limitless accessibility to users and potential customers, particularly so in areas of specific overlap. Ordinary consumers/users seeking to locate the functions available under one domain name may be confused if they accidentally arrive at a different but similar website which offers no such services. Such users could well conclude that the first domain name owner had misrepresented its goods or services through its promotional activities and the first domain owner would thereby lose customers. It is apparent therefore that a domain name may have all the characteristics of a trademark, which includes an action for passing off.

Distinction Between Trademark and Domain Name

There is, however, a distinction between a trademark and a domain name which is not relevant to the nature of the rights of an owner in connection with the domain name, but is material to the scope of the protection available to the right. The distinction lies in the manner in which the two operate. A trademark is protected by the laws of a country where such a trademark may be registered. Consequently, a trademark may have multiple registrations in many countries throughout the world. On the other hand, since the Internet allows for access without any geographical limitation, a domain name is potentially accessible irrespective of the geographical location of consumers. The outcome of this potential for universal connectivity is not only that a domain name would require worldwide exclusivity but also that national laws might be inadequate to effectively protect a domain name. The lacuna necessitated international regulation of the Domain Name System (DNS). This international regulation was effected through WIPO and ICANN. India is one of the 171 member states of WIPO, which was established as a vehicle for promoting the protection, dissemination and use of intellectual property throughout the world. Services provided by WIPO to its member states include the provision of a forum for the development and implementation of intellectual property policies internationally, through treaties and other policy instruments.

The outcome of consultation between ICANN and WIPO has resulted in the setting up of not only a registration system for domain names with accredited registrars but also the evolution of the Uniform Domain Name Disputes Resolution Policy (UDNDR Policy) by ICANN on October 24, 1999. Registration is provided on a first come first served basis.

As far as India is concerned, there is no legislation which explicitly refers to dispute resolution in connection with domain names. Although the operation of the Trade Marks Act, 1999 is not extra-territorial and may not allow for adequate protection of domain names. This does not mean that domain names are not to be legally protected to every extent possible under the laws relating to passing off.

The Court held that unless Satyam established goodwill by showing that the public associates the name Sify with Satyam, it could not succeed. After perusing the evidence provided by Satyam, the court held that it had been able to establish the nevessary goodwill and reputation. Apart from close visual similarity, there is phonetic similarity between the two names and the mere addition of 'net' to 'Siffy' does not detract from the similarity. Siffynet defended itself stating that 'Siffynet' was derived from a combination of the first letter of the five promoters of the company, namely Saleem, Ibrahim, Fazal, Fareed and Yusuf, and the word 'net' implies its business. The stand taken was that it was not aware of Satyam's trade name and trading style 'Sify'. Siffynet also argued that Satyam's 'Sify' was similar to other domain names such as Scifi.net, scifi.com etc. and that Sci-fi is used as an abbreviation of 'Science Fiction'. The court held that these arguments were incredible and ordered Siffynet not to use the disputed domain names.

There is no doubt that Siffynet adopted the mark after Satyam, which is the prior user and has the right to debar Siffynet from eroding the goodwill and reputation of Satyam.

This is a landmark judgment delivered at a time when Satyam had a good reputation and strong goodwill. The court held domain names to be an extension of trademark and provided protection under the existing law in Inida.

Now, let us examine how trademarks can be transferred in a will and what problems may arise in a family business using the same trademark in different geographical locations.

Haldiram Bhujiawala (Supreme Court of India, 2000)

This case highlights the importance of trademarks in business and how trademarks can be transferred by a will and how can it be commercially exploited by business partners. The facts of the case are very interesting and provide sufficient insight to understand these aspects.

Ganga Bishan, also known as Haldiram, has been doing business in the name of Haldiram Bhujiawala since 1941. In 1965, he constituted a partnership with his two sons—Moolchand, Shiv Kishan and his daughter-in-law Kamla Devi (wife of another son, RL Aggarwal) to carry on the business under the same name. In December 1972, the said firm applied for registration before the Registrar of Trademarks for registration of the name Haldiram Bhujiawala—Chand Mal—Ganga Bishan Bhujiawala, Bikaner. The Registrar of Trademarks granted registration with No. 285062. On 16 November, 1974, the partnership was dissolved and under the terms of the dissolution deed the above trademark fell exclusively to the share of Moolchand for the whole country except West Bengal. Kamla Devi was given ownership of the trademark rights for West Bengal. Lala Ganga Bishan Haldiram executed his last will, dated April 3, 1979, and also reiterated the rights conferred by the dissolution deed on the respective parties. He died in 1980. His will was later acted upon giving Moolchand the trademark rights for the entire country except West Bengal. Moolchand died in 1985 leaving behind his four sons—Shiv Kishan, Shiv Ratan, Manohar Lal, and Madhusoodan. All of them had their names recorded as subsequent joint proprietors.

The latter three formed a partnership in 1983 and started a shop in Chandni Chowk, New Delhi and sold various goods under the trademark of Haldiram Bhujiawala.

In the meantime, in 1977, Moolchand's brother RL Aggarwal (husband of Kamla Devi) and his son Prabhu Shankar, applied for registration in the name of Haldiram Bhujiawala at Kolkata claiming to be full owners of the said trademark without disclosing the dissolution deed dated November 16, 1974. When the Registrar objected on April 14, 1978, they replied on July 18, 1978, that they alone were trading in this name in Kolkata but they had no right to use the said trademark beyond Kolkata. The trademark was, in the usual course, renewed on December 29, 1986, until December

28, 1993. They also acquired a right on account of prior adoption and being a long user.

Kamla Devi had the ownership of the trademark rights for West Bengal. Her son Ashok Kumar constituted a new firm and opened a shop at Arya Samaj Road, Karol Bagh, New Delhi in the name of Haldiram Bhujiawala. He and his mother had no right to use this trademark outside West Bengal.

The Chandni Chowk shop owners came to know of it and objected to this development since Ashok Kumar and his mother Kamla Devi had the ownership of the trademark 'Haldiram Bhujiawala' only in West Bengal.

A dispute arose and the matter finally reached the Supreme Court. The court confined itself to a very limited question of law related to partnership and contract, yet it obliquely upheld that Kamla Devi and her son Ashok Kumar could not use the trademark 'Haldiram Bhujiawala' in Delhi as their ownership was restricted to West Bengal.

This case brings out the fundamental characteristics of intellectual property: that intellectual property can be transferred like any other property and its use is non-rivalrous, making it necessary to be vigilant about its use by competitors.

The following are two American cases—discussing the protection to a single colour and then to the concept of trade dress.

Qualitex v. *Jacobson* (US Supreme Court, 1995)

Qualitex sold dry cleaning press pads in a special shade of green-gold and registered this colour as a trademark. Its competitor, Jacobson, thereafter also started selling its press pads in a similar shade of green-gold. Qualitex challenged this in an infringement suit at the District Court where the judgment was in its favour. However, Jacobson challenged it in the Court of Appeals for the Ninth Circuit, which held that colour alone cannot be registered as a trademark. Against that judgment, Qualitex filed an appeal in the US Supreme Court. After discussing the provisions of the Lanham Act (the trademark law in the US) the Supreme Court held that colour alone could be registered as a trademark. The language of the Lanham Act describes trademarks in the broadest of terms and there is no mention that colour alone cannot be registered as a trademark.

Quaitex had argued that the green-gold they used had acquired secondary meaning and customers identified with the colour as used by Qualitex. Jacobson argued that colour for press pads served a definite function and therefore it should not be allowed to be registered as a trademark. The function of using a certain colour on press pads is to avoid noticeable stains. But the court held that using green-gold cannot be only functional, as any other colour could also be used equally effectively. Jacobson also argued that upholding the use of colour alone as a trademark would produce uncertainty and unresolvable court disputes about what shades of a colour a competitor may lawfully use and that there is only a limited supply of colours which will soon be depleted by competitors. The court did not agree with Jacobson's arguments.

This is a very interesting and important judgment and speaks volumes about the legal environment prevailing in the US. In one section it was mentioned, 'we do not see why courts could not apply those standards to a colour, replicating, if necessary, lighting conditions under which a coloured product is normally sold'. Such a reasoning may hold good in the US, however, it may not do so in India where one can argue that it is difficult to replicate such lighting conditions due to poor economic conditions, unavailability of adequate power in most of the cities in India and illiteracy in general. It can be agreed that such lighting conditions are created in garment shops or particularly in 'matching centres' where fabric of matching colours is bought and sold. These conditions can also be critical for selling paints where even white paint may be available in half a dozen different shades. In such a situation, it may be difficult to distinguish between two almost identical shades, which are 'technically' different. Would the courts allow both shades to be registered as trademarks? Or would the courts go with the basic concept of 'confusingly similar' or 'deceptively similar' colours. These questions have become more and more difficult to answer today, when tens of thousands of colours can be produced on the computer screen with the click of the mouse. What will happen in times to come? More and more disputes regarding trademarks for colours.

Two Pesos v. *Taco Cabana* (US Supreme Court, 1992)

Taco Cabana operates chain of fast food restaurants in Texas that serve Mexican food. The first restaurant was opened in 1978. It describes its Mexican trade dress as:

> [A] festive eating atmosphere having interior dining and patio areas decorated with artifacts, bright colours, paintings and murals. The patio includes interior and exterior areas, with the interior patio capable of being sealed off from the outside patio by overhead garage doors. The stepped exterior of the building is a festive and vivid colour scheme using top border paint and neon stripes. Bright awnings and umbrellas continue the theme.

In 1985, Two Pesos opened a restaurant in Houston and adopted a motif very similar to the description of Taco Cabana's trade dress. A year later, Taco Cabana entered the Houston and Austin markets where Two Pesos was already doing business. Taco

Cabana was shocked to find that its trade dress had been copied blatantly by Two Pesos. It filed a case which finally reached the US Supreme Court and it held that Taco Cabana's trade dress was inherently distinctive and there was no need to prove that it had acquired a secondary meaning and thus, Two Pesos was restrained from using the same trade dress.

This was a landmark judgment where the court had held that trade dress is an important intellectual property asset for any company, and the law would provide sufficient protection against infringers.

A similar case has been that of ITC Bukhara (the famous Delhi restaurant) and Bukhara Grill, a restaurant in Manhattan, New York. ITC Bukhara, Delhi, has been in business since 1977 and Bukhara Grill began its business in 1999 and copied the Delhi restaurant's logo, décor, staff uniforms, wood-slab menus, red-checkered customer bibs, pathani suits for waiters, even the names of the dishes. The New York restaurant had no affiliation with the Delhi restaurant. ITC filed a case in the American courts on the grounds that its trademark and trade dress had been copied and it was a case of passing-off. ITC lost the case as the American courts held that ITC did not have a US trademark registration. ITC argued that it was a 'famous or well-known' trademark, so even if it was not registered in the US, it must be granted protection. Ironically, the courts did not agree with this argument and held that though ITC Bukhara may be well-known in India, it did not have the requisite goodwill in New York and hence could not be given a well-known trademark status.

The following is a very recent case illustrating brand wars in advertisements and use of intellectual property rights as legal weapons against competitors.

HT Media v. *UTV News* (Calcutta High Court, 31 August, 2010)

Hindustan Times Media Limited is a well-known publisher of *The Hindustan Times*. A few years ago it launched a business daily called *Mint*, in collaboration with the world famous *The Wall Street Journal*. In May 2009, HT released a series of advertisements in the form of an announcement with a sentence which had only some of the words in English; the rest of the words were made up of Greek letters that may or may not constitute words in that language. HT started a high-profile publicity drive by launching the advertisement campaign in print media. The essential message was contained in the following slogan appearing at the bottom of the advertisement:

'Presenting *Mint*, refreshing clarity in business news.'

Below the slogan were two further lines in smaller print:

'Clear and well-analysed business minus the jargon.'

'Global perspective with an exclusive section from *The Wall Street Journal*. Every day.'

According to HT, the concept of incorporating the notion that ordinary business news as it was presented may be Greek to the audience, not well-versed in that old and rich language and its publication, namely '*Mint*', was different and the news that it communicated was lucid and easy to comprehend.

A television channel—Bloomberg UTV—started a rival series of advertisements. HT first noticed them in June 2010, in Delhi and Kolkata editions of a newspaper. The message in these advertisements started with four or five English words and the rest of the sentence in Greek. Towards the bottom of the advertisement it read as follows:

Let's face it. Business channels actually sound Greek to most of us. Which raises a rather interesting question. Why is it harder to understand money than to earn it? To be honest, it's not. At least not on Bloomberg UTV. We tell you things like they are. Straight, simple and uncomplicated.

HT's Contention

HT complained that UTV's advertisement was a blatant copy of its earlier advertisements. It insisted that in its conceptualization of the idea and the expression thereof in tangible form, it was entitled to the exclusive use of the manner of expression thereof and any variant of such expression would amount to infringement of its copyright. HT further said that its advertisement had achieved a trademark signification, thereby exclusively associating with HT—which had already received some awards for this advertisement. UTV had slavishly and unimaginatively copied the idea of depicting Greek words between English expressions. Such copying would create confusion and deception in the minds of the public who may presume a connection, collaboration or association of HT with UTV. Such conduct amounted not only to unfair trade practice but also to infringement of HT's intellectual property rights.

HT further argued in the court that it did not seek protection of any intangible idea but it asserted its exclusivity in the manner of expression of the concept that essentially involves English words to be juxtaposed against Greek letters or words to convey the sense that though business news may generally be perceived as being strange and incomprehensible, HT's product—*Mint*—was distinctive in its clarity of presentation. HT also said that this is a clear-cut case of passing-off. However, this was restricted to the advertisement and passing-off has not been claimed for the product of *Mint*.

UTV's Defence

UTV defended itself by saying that HT's intellectual property was confined only to a copyright in its series of advertisements and such advertisements did not have any artistic distinctiveness. UTV's expression in its advertisement was altogether different and it was free to make a statement that business news may be Greek to a reader or a viewer. UTV had chosen a complete sentence in each of its advertisements and had expressed the same theme by beginning the sentence in English and finishing it in Greek. Thus there was a fundamental difference in the expressions of HT's advertisements and UTV's advertisements, in that even if a person was well-versed in English and Greek, they would not be able to make any sense of the sentence written in HT's advertisement. However, if a person knew English and Greek, they could understand the sentence expressed in UTV's advertisement.

This is a very recent and interesting case of disparaging advertisements. The Kolkata High Court held that the theme or the idea of both the advertisements might be the same, however, as the expressions are different, HT could not get an injunction against UTV. Regarding the action of passing-off, the court held that passing-off is wide enough to encompass advertising campaigns but the fundamental basis of such action is that the advertising campaign has developed a goodwill that would lead the market to associate it with HT's product. In this instant case the court held that it was not the case, as HT's *advertisement* had not yet developed the requisite goodwill for this purpose.

In this judgment, there are several references to disparaging advertisements, mostly from the English courts. The law regarding disparaging advertisements is fast developing in India due to mushrooming TV channels, newspapers and other magazines. There is a very thin line between copying the concept or the basic theme of an advertisement and providing it a new expression. Often, there are retaliatory advertising campaigns by competing companies and more and more such cases will end up in courts of law. Intellectual property rights like copyrights and trademarks will provide the necessary tools and weapons to fight such cases in court. As these laws are being interpreted by the courts in a much more liberal manner, the dust will settle sooner than later regarding these advertisements. However, creativity of the mind will surely bring newer disputes. This is expected to happen more with advertisements on new mediums like the Internet and mobile telephones.

FOOD FOR THOUGHT

'Tata Sumo Industrial (R)', with an office at Tirupur, Tamil Nadu operates as a recruitment agency. It sends interview letters to unemployed persons and asks them to send money in the form of postage stamps. It has nothing to do with the famous Tata group in India. However, as it is named Tata Sumo, several unemployed persons, who desperately need a job, fall into the trap. This brings bad publicity to the Tata group. What should the Tata Group do?

FILL IN THE BLANKS

i) Trademarks are forever, however, they need to be _____.

ii) The MGM lion roar has been registered as a _____ mark.

iii) 'Water' cannot be granted as a trademark for_____.

TRUE OR FALSE

a) Even unregistered trademarks are protected under common law.

b) India has been more liberal as compared to the US in granting trademarks.

c) Foreign marks do not get any protection in India until and unless they are registered in India.

d) A bank like the the State Bank of India cannot get protection for its mark as it provides only service.

5

Designs

Have you ever tasted Britannia's 'Little Hearts' biscuits? They are in the shape of a heart and according to the company; they just melt in the mouth. The point of interest here is, will the biscuits not melt in the mouth if they are not shaped as a heart? Or, will the biscuits not taste the same if they are not in the shape of a heart? The answer to both the questions is 'no'. Then, what is the importance of shape here? Well, it is supposed to be unique and the company has got the shape registered as a design, with the registration No.165279. Similarly, other biscuit shapes have also been registered as a design.

Design does play a significant role in positioning of a product. The impact of a new design can be witnessed by the fact that Coca-Cola initiated a new design for its bottles and aluminum cans just to ensure that customers could easily hold the can and feel it colder for a longer time. The company came up with fantastic new designs and won the Grand Prix at Cannes Lions Award Programme in June 2008. A team of sixty designers—a mix of graphic and industrial, worked to make the aluminum contour bottle, which instead of can looks better, is easier to hold and feels colder for a longer time. These were called the 'Magnificent 5' or M5 and were featured at the world's most exclusive clubs and lounges.

SALIENT FEATURES

A design appeals solely to the eye. The eye must be the eye of the customer on a visual test. There should not be any functional consideration. Designs which are functional cannot be registered under the Designs Act. The purpose of this law is to provide protection to the originator of a new design so that he is not deprived of his reward if others apply his designs to their goods without his permission.

American law

The American Law on the subject is incorporated in the Patent Law and a design patent is granted for an aesthetic appearance of a product rather than its functional features. Design patents can be obtained for cars, televisions, refrigerators, monitors, tools, furniture, shoes, biscuits, etc. The scope is quite extensive. This law overlaps with Copyright and Trade Mark Law. The original law in the US was enacted in 1842 and it extended to 'new and original designs for articles of manufacture' and the purpose was to 'give encouragement to the decorative arts'.

Appearance is the crucial factor in design patent protection. The requirements are the same as those for patent protection namely; novelty, originality, non-obviousness, and it should be ornamental and not dictated by functional considerations. The novelty should be in the eyes of an 'ordinary observer' viewing the new design as a whole. He should not consider it to be a modification of an already existing design. The design should be non-obvious which requires the 'exercise of the inventive or originative faculty'. Such a design must be ornamental, creating a more pleasing appearance. It should be 'a product of aesthetic skill and artistic conception'. If a design is 'primarily functional rather than ornamental' it is not patentable.

It has been argued in the US that design registration is too expensive and it takes too long to obtain a design patent. In 1988 the cost of a design patent application was about US$1000. After more than twenty years this cost must have gone up at least ten times which may be a limiting factor for new designers.

Indian Law

In India, the Designs Act was passed in 1911 and since then a number of amendments have been made in the law. However, in the year 2000, the need was felt to have a new law instead of making any more amendments in the existing one. The Designs Act, 2000 was enacted and its basic purpose was to establish the new law in line with considerable progress made in the fields of science and technology. It is desirable that the law promotes design activity so that consumers get a better-made product which looks attractive and is pleasing to the eyes. In the absence of an effective law, infringement may be rampant and designers will have almost no incentive to initiate and develop new designs.

A design can be registered only when it is *new or original* and not previously published in India. It must be a new shape, configuration, pattern, or ornamentation or composition of lines or colours applied to such article in any form by an industrial process. It does not include any trade or property mark or artistic work. Protection is given to the design and not the article itself. Thus, the design must apply to an article. A combination of previously known designs can be registered if it produces a new visual appeal. To get registration, it should neither be published in a prior document nor be in prior use. The private, secret or experimental use of a new design shall not be considered as 'prior use'.

The design law overlaps with the trade mark and copyright law. If a design, which qualifies for registration under the Designs Act, has not been registered under the Designs Act, the exclusive right shall subsist under the copyright law. However, if such a design is commercially produced more than fifty times by an industrial process, the copyright shall cease to exist for any such design. Both copyright and design act protection cannot be granted coterminously. It has to be either of them. There is also a confusion and overlap between designs and trade mark which we shall examine in detail in the case discussed later in the chapter.

Tahiliani's case

Tarun Tahiliani is a well known fashion designer and enjoys global reputation. His work is highly regarded and is much in demand in elite fashion circles. He has his own company and employs a number of designers to work for him under his guidance. All the creative work is either done by him or by other designers for and on behalf of his company. All designing work is done under his guidance and detailed instructions. After designing, it is executed under his close supervision to result in the final product—the exclusive designer garment. The designers enter into a contract with his company and one of the primary clauses of the contract is that they agree to transfer the copyright of the new design to the employer, that is, Tahiliani's company.

It is a highly competitive field where designers of Tahiliani's repute work extremely hard to develop new designs. Due to exclusive designs, these are not mass produced. Very few pieces are made of any one single design and these pieces are exceedingly expensive. It is often very tempting for competitors to copy such designs and use them in dresses designed by them with slight modifications. Rajesh Masrani is Tahiliani's competitor and Tahiliani has complained that Masrani copied his work on several occasions. Masrani has not only copied the work partially but has gone to the extent of copying it fully and blatantly. Left with no other option, Tahiliani filed a case against Masrani in the Delhi High Court pleading for an order restraining Masrani from reproducing, printing, publishing, and distributing, selling or offering for sale, prints in any form, any colourable imitation or substantial reproduction of Tahiliani's fabric prints including the drawings and sketches.

Let us examine the law in this regard. The designs made by Tahiliani are protected under the copyright law which provides protection for artistic work provided that the article has not been reproduced more than fifty times. This is a copyright in the design. To get copyright protection, it is not necessary to have registration. Thus, Tahiliani gets a copyright protection for his design even if he did not opt for registration of such a design under copyright law. The question to be answered is whether Tahiliani's design can be registered under the Designs Act for which there is a new law in India, that is, the Designs Act, 2000. It says that there cannot be any design protection for an artistic work as mentioned in the Copyright Act. Hence, as Tahiliani's work is artistic work according to the copyright law, it cannot be registered as a design.

Masrani argued that Tahiliani neither applied for a design registration nor for copyright registration. Therefore, according to Masrani, Tahiliani had no protection given by law to his designs and Masrani was free to copy such designs.

Creation to Execution: The Six Steps

Tahiliani's work is executed on a finished garment from the creation of an artwork at his studio in the following six stages:

1. Pattern is created by Tahiliani or his designers on a computer till it becomes print-worthy.
2. The print is sent for 'swatching', that is, preliminary printing in actual size.
3. Swatches are evaluated and final changes are made. Thereafter, Tahiliani—with his team—freezes the final work and a master file is generated.
4. Samples are made with this master file. These samples are shown to prospective buyers and on their approval and feedback, orders are taken.
5. From the master file, production files are made. These are sent on a DVD to the Production Department, which in turn sends them to a specialized printer.
6. The specialized printer reproduces the final print on the fabric.

Tahiliani filed a comparative chart of a few of his works allegedly copied by Masrani, in the court. He argued that similarities between his work and Masrani's work were numerous and the reproduction by Masrani was *far too exact* to have been created independently. Masrani's work was *slavish reproduction* of his work. Such similarities suggested that Masrani had obtained access to Tahiliani's work in digital form. One of the comparative charts providing details from Tahiliani's Autumn Winter 2006–7 collection is as follows:

Tahiliani's Autumn Winter 2006–7 Collection

	Tahiliani's Work	Masrani's Work
1.	*Colour:* An Indo-western print characterized by the prominent use of the colours pinkish-orange and yellow.	An Indo-western print characterized by the prominent use of the colours pinkish-orange and yellow with some visible smudging/running of colour.
2.	*Central Motif:* The central motif is a glittering diamond/stone necklace with a large fiery-red ruby pendant in an asymmetrical shape in the centre and flanked by two smaller rubies on either side. The three rubies give off a unique impression of flowing into each other.	The central motif is a glittering diamond necklace with a large fiery-red ruby pendant in an asymmetrical shape in the centre and flanked by two smaller rubies on either side. The three rubies give off a unique impression of flowing into each other.
3.	Another string of diamond/stones follows the one on top, encircling a Mughal miniature painting in an oval, stone-studded frame, followed by a central pear-shaped motif encircling a kundan centerpiece and culminating in a ruby and stone teardrop.	Another string of diamond/stones follows the one on top, encircling a Mughal miniature painting in an oval, stone-studded frame, followed by a central pear-shaped motif encircling a kundan centerpiece and culminating in a ruby and stone teardrop.

4.	The second string of stones forms the line of demarcation for the two colours with the top one-quarter comprising a self-embossed yellow and the bottom three-quarters comprising symmetrical vertical columns of an overall orangish-pink hue.	The second string of stones forms the line of demarcation for the two colours with the top one-quarter comprising a self-embossed yellow and the bottom three-quarters comprising symmetrical vertical columns of an overall orangish-pink hue.
5.	The columns in the bottom three-quarters contain intricate patterns of interwoven Indian floral motifs that are repeated in four-column symmetry.	The columns in the bottom three-quarters contain intricate patterns of interwoven Indian floral motifs that are repeated in four-column symmetry.
6.	The overall impression is that of a uniquely different image with a number of intricately woven elements fused together with a creative flair and resulting in an overall print that is part-asymmetrical and fanciful and part-systematic and orderly; but wholly new.	The overall impression is that of an identical, poorly disguised and poorly executed copy with no attempt at originality; with the sole intent of reaping the fruits of Tahiliani's creative labour.

Tahiliani alleged that Masrani somehow had access to the DVD of the production file and it was from that file that he had been able to copy Tahliniani's work to the last detail. Masrani did not categorically deny infringement of copyright. However, he said that Tahiliani's designs were not original, were not registered, and hence, did not deserve protection in the eyes of the law.

The Delhi High Court held that this was a straightforward case of piracy of copyright in design and it was not at all necessary to have registration of such a copyright. Thus Tahiliani had the protection provided by law to his work and Masrani was liable for infringing such a copyright.

This is a very interesting case and provides necessary relief to high profile designers whose work is highly regarded and imitation can be immensely harmful to them and their business. Such a protection was always available under the law. However, the new law that is the Designs Act, 2000, provides that an artistic work cannot be registered as a design and hence such designs will get protection under the law if no more than fifty copies are made. Earlier to get such a protection, it was necessary to get it registered under the design law which itself is a tedious and time consuming process. As registration of copyright is not compulsory, any designer gets a copyright on his work, the moment the work is finished. It gives great relief to all such creative persons who do not have time and energy to follow up and coordinate regularly with the designs' office to get a registration. The Delhi High Court has also given a positive signal that the interpretation of law and the mood of judiciary are in the interest of creativity and the courts shall not allow any copying. In cases of prima facie instances of flagrant copying, the courts shall not shy away from granting a temporary injunction. Had there been very few similarities in this case, the final decision of the court might have been different. But in cases of 'slavish reproduction' of the original work, the court will definitely pass an injunction order restraining the imitator from taking benefit of copying. Originality ultimately wins!

Corning Case

This is a judgment which deals with the controversy between Corning (US) and an Indian seller. Corning was selling ophthalmic blanks to be used in spectacles. These were used by opticians and as these are meant for correcting visions, the blanks did not bear the Corning brand name or mark. Absence of any such name or mark on the blanks provided tremendous scope for copying and passing off inferior goods. Corning along with other manufacturers, Schott of Germany and Pilkington from the UK adopted a method of distinguishing 'the blanks' by engraving fine lines on the outer periphery of the blanks, protruding mildly. These fine lines were called 'edge lungs, lines or ribs'. These provided an easy mechanism to distinguish Corning products. Corning was making products with 3 and 5 ribs, Schott was making with 1 rib and Pilkington was making with 2 and 4 ribs.

Pilkington assigned all its rights to Corning and thus Corning got rights for 2, 3, 4, and 5 rib products. These ribs were purely functional. No aesthetic or design aspects were present.

Corning was shocked to find that ophthalmic blanks and finished lenses bearing two ribs were already being marketed in Delhi. Investigation revealed that these were being manufactured in China and traders in Delhi were sourcing them from China and selling them in Delhi. Such a practice was quite common and traders were indulging in it unabashedly.

Corning tried to negotiate with one such seller—Raj Kumar Garg—to stop selling such Chinese products, to which Garg replied that the presence of such ribs could only be given recognition as a 'design' which Garg had already got registered for two ribs in the office of the Controller of Patents and Design, Kolkata. Corning argued that it was not a design but a 'trademark' and it had already filed for trademark registration for 3 and 5 ribs which was pending in the Trademarks Registry. Pilkington was selling its 2 and 4 ribs all over the world including India but did not file for a trademark protection. Thus Corning argued that it should get trademark protection for two rib products and there was no question of opting for design protection.

Corning took the matter to the Delhi High Court. The court observed that the fundamental difference between a trademark and design is that the former signals to the mind, the source or identity of the manufacturer of the article whereas the latter appeals to the eye and attracts the consumer. The court found that the two ribs on the periphery of the blanks are trademark. Moreover, once the spectacles are ready these ribs get concealed under the frame of the spectacles, therefore, '. . . the two ribs in question which do not appeal to the eye at all and are not capable of attracting a purchaser in any manner for the purchase thereof are not covered with the definition of design and are a trademark which is being used and adopted for connecting them with the producers thereof.'

The court held that Garg and others were free to source ophthalmic blanks from China but they have no right to confuse and mislead the customer with regard to the trademark. The court restrained Garg and others from selling such two rib blanks.

This is a very important and interesting judgment because there can be confusion between trademark and design as they are overlapping intellectual property protection and a company may like to opt for both such protections. However a company cannot use the same mark or a peculiar design for a trademark as well as design protection. The moment there is a functional element involved, the design aspect goes away.

Veet's S-shaped Spatula

Reckitt Benckiser launched the Veet hair removal system in India in 2004. This was marketed in modern soft squeezing tubes which was more hygienic than the jars that ordinary creams were marketed in. Veet came up with a large S-shaped spatula which was known as 'perfect touch' spatula or perfect touch tool. This spatula allowed easy application of cream and enabled a close contact with the skin during application and removal which resulted in perfect hair removal. Reckitt Benckiser obtained a design registration for this spatula with No. 193988 in December 2003.

Wyeth, which sells 'Anne French', another hair removal product offered a similar spatula and according to Reckitt Benckiser, Wyeth copied its design and thus infringed the copyright in the design of the spatula. Earlier, Anne French was selling with a flat spatula. Reckitt Benckiser alleged that there were a number of similarities between Veet spatula and Anne French spatula and thus pleaded in the Delhi High Court that Wyeth should be restrained from selling Anne French with the S-shaped spatula.

Wyeth pleaded in the court that Reckitt Benckiser's design was not new as it had already been registered in the UK, the US, and Australia. Moreover, Wyeth spatula had been advertised in print and audio-visual media as per information given by an advertising agency in Amsterdam and this was done well before December 2003. Also the spatula was advertised by Wyeth in an Australian magazine titled, 'Girlfriend' in December 2000. The spatula was quite obvious and was clearly shown in the photographs of such advertisements. Thus, Wyeth argued that Reckitt Benckiser's spatula had already been published earlier and was lacking in novelty.

The legal position to get a design registration is that there should not be any prior publication which includes prior registration or prior use.

Wyeth filed a comparative chart showing the differences between Anne French spatula and Veet spatula.

	Anne French Spatula	Veet Spatula
1.	*Contours:* It has substantially curved contours.	It has substantially angular and broad contours.
2.	*Outer Lines:* The outer lines of the spatula are broad at the ends and waisted in the middle.	The outer lines of the spatula are totally straight.
3.	*Shape:* The spatula is roughly of an 'hourglass' shape with a straight base portion, waisted middle and relatively wider upper portion.	The spatula is roughly of a 'U' shape. It has an increasing taper from the lower end to the upper end.
4.	*Front and back:* There are two crescent shaped indentations on the scoop part facing up and two on the reverse.	There are three horizontal lines in the front and three horizontal lines in the back of the spatula at the centre.

After examining the documents submitted by both parties, the Delhi High Court decided that Wyeth spatula was already registered in several foreign countries and hence it comes under the category of prior publication. It, therefore, does not deserve design registration. The court also observed that once a design is registered in India, it is made open to the public. It is not a secret document. However, the situation in the UK and perhaps in some other countries is a little bit different. The UK law allows two types of design registrations; (i) registrations which are open to the public and (ii) registrations which are secret. It is therefore obvious that registration by itself in the UK shall not amount to disclosure to the public as understood in the Indian context. But, as far as the Indian law is concerned, there is no doubt that once there is a registration, it is deemed to have been published and is open to public. The court also decided that because of such registrations, Wyeth spatula was already published abroad prior to the date of registration in India. Hence such a registration should not be allowed to continue.

Besides these questions of registration, the court also decided that observing both the spatula—Veet's and Anne French's—when kept side by side, it is difficult to say conclusively that one is the imitation of the other. Thus, Wyeth was allowed to sell Anne French with its S-shaped spatula.

This decision highlights the importance of a design and how companies can use the Designs Law as a legal tool to achieve competitive advantage. However, to do so, it is essential that such a company should go to the court with 'clean hands'. In this case, Reckitt Benckiser did not go to the court with clean hands as it did not reveal prior registrations done in foreign countries and also it did not reveal such information while filing for registration of its S-shaped spatula in the office of the Controller of Design.

The message is loud and clear—in order to get the benefit from law, one has to be on the right side of law and comply with the law in totality.

FOOD FOR THOUGHT

SCRABBLE was invented by Alfred Mosher Butts in the US and the trademark 'SCRABBLE' has been used since 1948. Hasbro owns the trademark in the US and Canada and Mattel owns it in the rest of the world. Jayant and his brother launched an online version of their board game SCRABULOUS as an application available on facebook.com. They also promoted scrabulous.com, scrabulous.info and scrabulous.org. Mattel filed a case against Jayant brothers, who alleged that there was no design registration for SCRABBLE and the copyright protection in any such design would have lasted only for fifteen years. What do you think would have been the outcome?

FILL IN THE BLANKS

i) Design appeals _____ to the eye.

ii) A design can be registered in India only when it is new or _____.

iii) In fashion designing, _____ is preliminary printing in actual size.

iv) Designs which are _____ cannot be registered under the Designs Act.

v) The design law overlaps with the _____ and _____.

TRUE OR FALSE

a) Design protection is provided for functional utility.

b) Prior publication is a necessary condition to get design registration.

c) The term of design protection is shorter than that of patent protection.

d) Design protection is not available for confectionery products. key to fill in the blanks

KEY TO FILL IN THE BLANKS

i)   Solely
ii)   Original
iii)   Swatching
iv)   Functional
v)   Trademark Copyright law

TRUE FALSE

a)   False
b)   False
c)   True
d)   False

6

Geographical Indications and Traditional Knowledge

Have you ever been offered a 'Tirupathi Laddu' prasadam from the famous Tirupathi temple? If you haven't, you must have heard about it. The laddu is almost synonymous with the temple, as each devotee receives only one laddu as prasadam. There is a huge gap between demand and supply, giving opportunity to unscrupulous businesspersons to sell similar-looking, ordinarily made laddus in the name of Tirupathi. Since 2009, it has become impossible to sell any laddu as a Tirupathi Laddu, because the laddu has been extended protection under India's Geographical Indications Law (GI). It was registered as GI Application No. 121, Class 30, with the Geographical Indications Registry in Chennai. Tirumala Tirupati Devasthanam (TTD), being the registered proprietor for the Tirupathi Laddu.

Similarly, Dusseheri mangoes from the Malihabad region near Lucknow have been registered as GI Application No. 125. Darjeeling Tea, and the logo used to identify it, were registered as GI application Nos. 1 and 2 in 2004, during the initial years of the registry.

SALIENT FEATURES

A geographical indication denotes that a product originates from a particular place and has a reputation for certain features linked to that particular place. Geographical indication identifies certain goods being agricultural, natural, or manufactured—that have originated or have been manufactured in the territory of a particular country, or a region or a locality. It is because of this geographical location that such goods possess certain essential characteristics. It is not at all necessary that the name of the product includes the name of that geographical territory.

TRIPS AND GI

Under the TRIPS Agreement (Agreement on Trade Related Aspects of Intellectual Property Rights), member countries are under an obligation to extend protection to a particular geographical indication provided it is protected in the country of its origin. Article 22 states that all member countries must provide legal protection to GIs in that country so as to prevent misuse of these marks for misleading the public. Article 23 provides this protection for wines and spirits.

LAW IN INDIA

The Indian law extends the protection to agricultural and manufactured products. Generally, such protection is extended to agricultural products which typically have qualities attributed to a specific geographical area and are influenced by factors such as climate, soil, water, etc. In India, there was no law for protection of such geographical indications until 'The Geographical

Indications of Goods (Registration and Protection) Act, 1999, was passed. It was obligatory under TRIPS, that unless a geographical indication is protected in its country of origin, it cannot receive reciprocal protection in other countries. So, even if India did not have a GI law to protect its own GIs, it was obliged to extend geographical indication protection to products from other countries. The same protection would not have been given to Indian GIs, as Indian law did to provide for any such protection. Thus, it was in India's interest to come up with the required law to provide GI protection to a large number of wonderful products in a country of continental size and a very long history. The law, enacted in 1999, came into force on September 15, 2003. Since then, a Geographical Indications Registry has been set up in Chennai and a good number of products have been registered. The first was Darjeeling Tea and its logo. Some other examples are Kancheevaram silk and Kolhapuri footwear. Geographical Indications do not belong to any single individual, but to an association of persons, producers or any organization or authority established by law. It must represent the interest of the producers of goods concerned. Registration is generally for a period of ten years and can be renewed. No other person or organization from any other part of the country or world can claim to have manufactured or produced such goods.

Registration of a GI is not compulsory to get protection. Even unregistered GIs get the protection of the common law of passing off, however, it is always advisable to register a GI because such registration is the best prima facie evidence in case of any infringement. GIs cannot be registered as a trademark. If it is, it cannot be registered as a GI. There are thirty four different GI classes under which goods can be registered, and the same item can be registered in more than one class. For example, woollen shawls from a particular region may be registered as wool from that region and also as embroidery.

THE AMERICAN LAW

The United States protects geographical indications as trademarks and such protection is more than the TRIPS Agreement requires. The United States has provided TRIPS-plus levels of protection to geographical indications of either domestic or foreign origin since 1946. A couple of examples are Florida oranges, Idaho potatoes and Washington State apples.

There are certain benefits of protecting geographical indications through the trademark system. One of the foremost advantages is that a trademark is already known to businesses. No additional resources are required by the government, and the trademark system accommodates geographical indications which are not only place names, but words, slogans, designs, three-dimensional marks, colours or even sounds and scents.

The American Law provides that geographical names can be registered as certification marks. A certification mark is any word, name, symbol, or device used by someone other than the owner of the mark to certify some aspects of the third party's goods or public services. The same mark can be used to certify more than one characteristics of the goods/services in more than one certification category: the mark Roquefort (US Registration No. 571798) is used to indicate that the cheese has been manufactured from sheep's milk and cured in the caves of the Community of Roquefort (France) in accordance with their long established methods and processes.

There are two major differences between trademarks and certification marks. First, the owner does not use a certification mark. Second, it does not indicate the commercial source and does not distinguish the services of one person from those of another. This means that any entity which meets the certifying standards is entitled to use a certification mark. A certification mark may not be used by the owner because the owner does not produce the goods or perform the services in connection with the mark used. The purpose of the certification mark is to inform purchasers that the goods/services of the authorized user possess certain characteristics or meet certain standards.

In the US, it is a government body that controls the use of a geographical term as a certification mark. There are two basic concerns; namely, preserving the freedom of all persons in the region to use it and prevent abuse of the mark, and that all applications are examined at the US Patent and Trademark Office (USPTO). If producers understand a sign to refer only to goods produced in a particular region and nowhere else, the sign functions as a regional certification mark. For instance, Cognac has been held to be a geographical indication for brandy originating in the Cognac region of France, and not to brandy produced elsewhere in France.

Geographical indications can also be protected as collaborative marks, which are marks adopted by associations, unions, cooperatives, etc., for use only by its members, who in turn use the mark to identify their goods and distinguish them from those of non-members. Collective marks indicate the commercial origin of goods. This law is more or less similar to the law regarding PDO in Europe and geographical indication in India.

EUROPEAN LAW OF PROTECTED DESIGNATION OF ORIGIN

European protection of 'geographical indications and designations of origin' was instituted as Council Regulation (EEC) No. 2081/92 of July 14, 1992, which came into force on July 24, 1993. It created a procedure by which the Commission can register a name which satisfies specified criteria as a 'Protected Designation of Origin' (PDO) or a 'Protected Geographical Indication' (PGI). A PDO is the name of a place used to describe a product, originating in that place, with characteristics that are due to its particular environment. A PGI is similar to a PDO except that the causal link between the place of origin and the quality of the product may be a matter of reputation rather than verifiable fact. The PDO is a form of intellectual property right, conferring upon producers in a certain area the exclusive right to use their regional name as descriptive of the product. That exclusive right, like all intellectual property rights, is inherently restrictive of trade. The exercise of that right is linked to strict requirements designed to ensure that the product conforms to established standards. PDOs provide very strong protection for the reputation of regional foods as they eliminate unfair competition and the misleading of consumers by non-genuine products or producers whose products may be of inferior quality or different flavour, by which the reputation of the original product may suffer.

France uses a system of 'Appellation d'origine contrôlée' (AOC), which translates as 'Controlled Designation of Origin'. It is the French certification granted to certain French GIs for wines, cheese, butter, etc. The system was introduced in 1919, and in 1925, Roquefort became the first cheese to be granted the AOC label.

An appellation of origin denotes the geographical environment, including natural and human factors. However, GIs may not have the qualities and characteristics exclusively due to the geographical environment. These are called GIs because they come from that geographical area. Thus, it can be said that 'all appellations of origin are GIs but not all GIs are appellations of origin'. Appellations of origin are a subset of GIs.

Scotch Whisky

This is a very interesting case, in which a United Kingdom manufacturers' association has taken the matter to the Delhi High Court and sought protection for Geographical Indication. The Scotch Whisky Association is registered as a company in the United Kingdom and has been incorporated with the object of protecting and promoting the interests of the Scotch whisky trade both in the United Kingdom and abroad.

For such protection, the Scotch Whisky Act, 1988 and the Scotch Whisky Order, 1990 have been enacted in the United Kingdom. The latter defines Scotch whisky as follows:

'Scotch whisky' means whisky—

(a) which has been produced at a distillery in Scotland from water and malted barley (to which only whole grains of other cereals may be added) all of which have been
   (i) processed at that distillery into a mash;
   (ii) converted to a fermentable substrate only by endogenous enzyme systems; and
   (iii) fermented only by the addition of yeast;
(b) which has been distilled at an alcoholic strength by volume of less than 94.8 percent so that the distillate has an aroma

and taste derived from the raw materials used in, and the method of, its production;

(c)   which has been matured in an excise warehouse in Scotland in oak casks of a capacity not exceeding 700 litres, the period of that maturation being not less than three years;

(d)   which retains the colour, aroma, and taste derived from the raw materials used in, and the method of, its production and maturation; and

(e)   to which no substance other than water and spirit caramel has been added.

It is quite clear from this definition that even in Scotland, all whisky produced need not necessarily fall within the definition of Scotch whisky.

Scotch whisky is known worldwide as a whisky produced in Scotland and is advertised as such. Taking advantage of such a strong reputation of Scotch whisky, Golden Bottling Limited, Bhiwadi, Rajasthan, started selling its whisky under the name 'Red Scot'. Apparently the purpose was to confuse the customers by giving an impression that it was Scotch whisky. When the Scotch Whisky Association found out about it, they sent a letter, and later a legal notice to Golden Bottling in 2000, advising it not to use the word 'Scot'. Golden Bottling did not reply. Left with no other option, the Scotch Whisky Association filed the case in the Delhi High Court on the grounds that Scotch whisky is a geographical indication in the United Kingdom and even if it is not registered as such in India, it is nonetheless protected under law, forbidding Golden Bottling from passing off its whisky as Scotch. The Scotch Whisky Association petitioned the Court to order Golden Bottling to refrain from using the word 'Scot', but no one made an appearance on behalf of potentially infringing bottler. The Court held that the reputation of Scotch whisky has been irreparably damaged by the use of the word 'Scot' in whisky manufactured by Golden Bottling, whose whisky is not in fact Scotch whisky. Thus the Court awarded damages to the tune of Rs 5 lakhs and another Rs 3 odd lakhs for litigation costs.

This is one of those cases where it is obvious that one of the parties is taking advantage of the very strong reputation of another's product. In the absence of any protection provided by the Geographical Indications Act, the Indian party could have gone ahead and kept selling its goods. However, the trademark law or the common law action of passing off a product as another would have provided legal remedy to the foreign party. This would not have necessarily provided an affective remedy to the foreign party in the absence of strong interpretation of the existing law in favour of intellectual property protection. Such protection has been provided and thus made stronger by proper and timely enactment of intellectual property laws in India. This has been possible because India is a signatory of TRIPS and is under an obligation to update its intellectual property laws.

Parma Ham

Parma is a city in Italy famous for its ham, cheese, architecture, fine countryside, and the University of Parma, one of the oldest universities in the world. Parma ham is made in the Parma area, from pigs reared in northern and central Italy and is famous throughout the world. It is made according to traditional methods and standards and is a PDO (Protected Designation of Origin) under Italian and European Community Law. The guarantee of authenticity is the brand's mark in the form of a five-pointed coronet—corona ducale. Under Italian law, this has to appear on the product in whatever form—complete ham, slices, prepackaged pieces, or slices—when sold to the customer. The name 'Parma ham' and the trademark can only be used by the Parma Ham Association, which has its own system of inspection and supervision. No other manufacturer or seller can use the name Parma ham. Also, ham produced anywhere else in the world cannot be called Parma ham.

Under Italian law, the designation 'Parma ham' is protected by Law No. 26 of February, 1990: 'Protection of denomination of origin Prosciutto di Parma'.

Article 1 provides that the designation is exclusively reserved for, '. . . ham equipped with a distinguishing mark that allows permanent identification, obtained by processing fresh legs of national pigs...produced according to the provisions laid down in this law and aged in the traditional area of production. . .'

Article 6 deals with the application of the mark:

1. After the mark has been applied, Parma ham can be sold deboned and in pieces of varying weight and shape, or it may be sliced and suitably packaged.
2. In cases provided for in sub-paragraph 1, if it is not possible to keep the mark on the product, the former shall be indelibly stamped so that it cannot be removed from the packaging, under the control of the competent body and according to methods determined in the statutory instruments. In these cases, packaging operations shall be carried out in the traditional production area. . .

Parma Ham Sold by Hygrade Foods

Hygrade Foods is a British company that imports boned hams from a producer in Parma, Italy. Indisputably, these hams are authentic, properly made, and branded. Hygrade slices and packages these hams in England. These packages are described as Parma Ham but they do not bear 'the five-pointed cornet'. The Parma Ham Association alleges that Hygrade's slicing and packaging is unlawful under Italian and European Law, which is enforceable in the courts of all member states. The Parma Ham Association calls for restraining Hygrade from marketing the packages as Parma ham.

This is a very interesting conflict of laws, where Italian law definitely provides that ham which has been sliced and packaged in England cannot be called Parma ham and therefore cannot be provided a brand mark of the five-pointed coronet. However, the European law applicable in England may provide otherwise, and can only be resolved by analysing the European law and getting the proper interpretation from the British Courts. Until that time there was no conflict between the Italian and British law. The British Courts, after looking into the matter, raised certain questions and provided some illustrations. What follows is one of the more interesting ones:

Consider, also, the case of a restaurant or delicatessen. A restaurant buys a leg of Parma ham, duly stamped with the corona ducale, slices it in the restaurant kitchen and, on its menu, offers Parma ham with melon. It would be absurd to suppose that this was a process that the product specification was intended to control. If a delicatessen purchases a leg of Parma ham, cuts some slices off the ham and places those slices in its front counter with a label 'Parma Ham', is that a process the product specification is intended to control? The Court observed that the answer to this question would be: 'Obviously not'.

Consider this again. If Parma ham, eligible to be so described because it was sold on the bone, or boneless, with the corona ducale stamp, is sliced by the restaurateur and offered to the public in slices described in the menu as Parma ham, the slices must surely have the same eligibility as the leg from which they were sliced. And if the proprietor of a delicatessen slices the Parma ham in a back room and places the slices under his glass counter with a label declaring them to be Parma ham, the argument that the slicing and labelling have deprived the product of its eligibility to be described as Parma ham seems a very difficult one to accept.

The British courts eventually referred the matter to the European Court of Justice to decide whether the PDO Parma Ham 'Prosciutto di Parma' created a valid community right, directly enforceable in the court of a member state, to restrain the retail sale as 'Parma ham' of sliced and packaged ham derived from hams duly exported from Parma in compliance with the conditions of the PDO, but which have not been thereafter sliced, packaged and labeled in accordance with the specification.

Doctrine of Exhaustion of Rights

The doctrine of exhaustion of rights has been developed by the European Court in relation to national intellectual property rights. The European Court has held that where a proprietor of an intellectual property right relating to goods has put the goods into free circulation, the proprietor cannot rely on the intellectual property right in order to prevent resale of the goods.

Basmati

'Basmati' means 'aroma filled'. Basmati rice is famous for its aroma and post-cooking elongation—more than twice its original length. The combination of these two features is not found in any other strain of rice. Basmati rice has become a delicacy all over the world, but it is only grown in India and Pakistan. In India, it has been cultivated at the foot of the Himalayan mountain ranges since times immemorial. The Basmati paddy fields of Haryana and Punjab are irrigated by the Yamuna and Sutluj rivers respectively. The old Karnal district, known as the 'rice bowl of India' provides the best quality Basmati in India. Basmati is now grown in the Karnal, Panipat, Kaithal, Kurukshetra, and Ambala districts of Haryana. It is also grown in Punjab, the Dehradun region of Uttarakhand and the Jammu region of Jammu & Kashmir.

RiceTec, a Texas-based, American rice company uses the latest technology to produce better quality and high-value products. It is one of the first companies to commercialize hybrid rice seed in North and South America. RiceTec filed for a patent for Basmati rice at the USPTO. The details are as follows:

Basmati Patent Details

A patent application was made for 'Basmati Rice Lines And Grains' by way of Application No. 272353 filed on July 8, 1994, by RiceTec, Inc. Alvin, Texas. The patent for the same was granted on September 2, 1997 as US Patent No. 5663484. The abstract of the patent application reads as follows:

> The invention relates to novel rice lines and to plants and grains of these lines and to a method for breeding these lines. The invention also relates to a novel means for determining the cooking and starch properties of rice grains and its use in identifying desirable rice lines. Specifically, one aspect of the invention relates to novel rice lines whose plants are semi-dwarf in stature, substantially photoperiod insensitive and high yielding, and produce rice grains having characteristics similar or superior to those of good quality basmati rice. Another aspect of the invention relates to novel rice grains produced from novel rice lines. The invention provides a method for breeding these novel lines. A third aspect of the invention relates to the finding that the 'Starch Index' (SI) of a rice grain can predict the grain's cooking and starch properties, to a method based thereon for identifying grains that can be cooked to the firmness of traditional basmati rice preparations, and to the use of this method in selecting desirable segregants in rice breeding programs.

The Dispute

RiceTec tried to enter the international Basmati market with brands similar to it like 'Kasmati' and 'Texmati' describing them as Basmati-type rice, but this strategy did not achieve much success. After being granted the patent in 1997, RiceTec was given the right to use the word 'Basmati' for its rice in the US, and also the right to label its export carton with the name 'Basmati'. Basmati patent rights gave RiceTec Inc. the exclusive right over the Basmati name. This new development in the international Basmati market caused grave repercussions for India and Pakistan because India would have lost out on thousands of tonnes of exports to the US, and also its position in crucial markets in Europe and the Middle East.

A couple of NGOs from India fought the matter in the US and demanded an amendment of US rice standards to specify that the word 'basmati' can be used only for rice grown in India and Pakistan on the grounds it was a geographical indication and even if grown elsewhere, rice cannot be called 'Basmati'. In 2000, the Basmati patent was officially challenged by the Government of India on technical grounds of novelty, usefulness and non-obviousness. An application for patent re-examination was filed before the USPTO by the Indian government through Agricultural and Processed Food Exports Development Authority (APEDA) after gathering required evidence.

It took a while for the Indian Government to gather all the evidence that would nullify claims made in the patent. The evidence proved that all claims made by RiceTec with regard to Basmati rice already existed in the Basmati rice produced in India. On the other hand, RiceTec and the US Rice Federation argued that Basmati was a generic word used for all aromatic rice and not particularly for rice grown in India and Pakistan.

India challenged three claims numbered 15, 16, and 17 of RiceTec's patent, which described the grain quality as aroma and elongation in cooking. RiceTec, on its own, removed these claims and the USPTO further struck down others. Thus, RiceTec's patent was left with very few claims, none of which were threatening for Basmati.

This was a major victory for India.

PRECAUTIONS TO BE TAKEN BY OWNERS OF GIs

In case the owner of a GI gets the product registered in India, it is equally important to get it registered or protected by whatever legal systems are provided in neighbouring countries like Pakistan, Bangladesh, Sri Lanka, Nepal, Bhutan, Maldives, Myanmar, etc. India is a very big market in this region and there is always the temptation and possibility to have counterfeit products manufactured in these countries and then exported to India. Thus, it is essential to have protection—by registration or otherwise—in India and neighbouring countries.

It is also important to register the GIs as domain names. For instance, www.darjeelingtea.com is a registered domain name and is owned by the Darjeeling Tea Association with its registered office in Kolkata and branch office in Darjeeling. There is also a circular logo depicting a woman smelling tea leaves with 'Darjeeling Tea' written in an arch at the top and the tag line 'No Flavour Finer' in a straight line at the bottom. Regarding Basmati rice, the website www.basmati.com is also registered. Other examples are www.champagne.fr for Champagne and www.scotchwhisky.com for Scotch whisky.

Owners must be vigilant and protect their GIs against unauthorized use by sending a 'cease and desist notice' when required, and later initiating civil and/or criminal action if necessary.

TRADITIONAL KNOWLEDGE

Traditional knowledge is passed on from one generation to the next, mostly in oral form and sometimes in writing. This knowledge comprises innovations, information, practices, customs, traditions, etc. The knowledge may be with regard to the use of natural resources, environment, plants and animals, curing diseases or nature in general. Most of this knowledge is undocumented. It is possible—though not in legal manner—to receive a patent for any traditional knowledge by not disclosing the knowledge to the patent office. In case the patent office does not have information about such knowledge, or the office tries to search but fails to find any mention or documentation of such knowledge, the patent office may grant the patent. For instance, the use of neem in India is very common, but may not be documented. Taking advantage of this fact, it had been patented in the US. This is a clear-cut case of stealing traditional knowledge from India and patenting it in one's own name. This is wrong—both legally and ethically. This practice is called 'Bio-piracy'. Let us examine the cases of neem and turmeric, which were patented in the US.

Neem

The neem tree is very common in India and its uses are many. From pest control to curing cold and flu, from skin diseases to dental care, neem is simply ubiquitous. For Indians, neem is an integral part of life. An American company, WR Grace and the US Department of Agriculture received a patent, No. 436257 in 1994 from the European Patent Office, for a method of controlling fungi in plants by using neem oil. It was opposed by India on the grounds that such knowledge was freely available for centuries in India and due documentary evidence was presented, leading the European Patent Office to revoke the patent in 2000. The patentees appealed in 2006, and were rejected.

Thus, traditional knowledge is very valuable and it is in the interest of everyone to document it, preferably in electronic form, so it can be searched by patent offices worldwide.

Another interesting case was turmeric, which is a very commonly used spice in Indian kitchens.

Turmeric

Turmeric is used as a spice in kitchens and also as medicine for several ailments in India. It is used to heal wounds and also in cosmetics. The USPTO granted patent No. 5401504 in 1995 to Suman K Das and Hari Har P Cohly, working at the University of Mississippi Medical Centre for using turmeric for healing wounds. In India through, the Council of Scientific & Industrial Research (CSIR), opposed it on the grounds it was prior knowledge, as it was commonly known in India for ages and hence, it lacked novelty. Texts in Sanskrit were produced as evidence. The patent was revoked in 1997, making it a very important victory for India.

TRADITIONAL KNOWLEDGE DIGITAL LIBRARY

Had the information about turmeric and neem been documented in electronic form and also available to patent offices conducting the patent search, it would not have been possible to award the patents in the first place. Lack of such searchable knowledge provides an opportunity to people like Das and Cohly and companies like WR Grace to patent things which are already common knowledge of the people. This is like reinventing the wheel. There have been efforts after such incidents to document traditional knowledge in India—by no means an easy task—which is available in dozens of languages and scores of dialects.

FOOD FOR THOUGHT

France produces dozens of cheeses, which once prompted Charles de Gaulle to make the statement: 'How can anyone govern a nation that has two hundred and forty six different kinds of cheese?' India has dozens and dozens of different kinds of mangoes—some very particular in taste and belonging to a very specific region—that it may become quite difficult for a layman (not a connoisseur of mangoes) to differentiate between very similar mangoes. Do you think it is a good idea to grant GI status to all of them? The same may be true for bananas, oranges, apples, laddus, samosas, teas, coffees, etc.

FILL IN THE BLANKS

i)   A GI signals to the consumer the _____ where the product has been made.

ii) The law for GI in _____ is older than that of the United States.

iii) It is important to _____ traditional knowledge to prevent its patenting elsewhere.

TRUE OR FALSE

a) GI is a subset of Appellations of Origin.

b) All whisky made in Scotland is called 'Scotch Whisky'.

c) The term of GI protection cannot be renewed.

d) Traditional knowledge only refers to knowledge which has been preserved for generations in written form.

KEY TO FILL IN THE BLANKS

i)   Place

ii)   Europe

iii) Document

TRUE FALSE

a)   False

b)   False

c)   False

d)   False

7

Trade Secrets and Confidential Information

The movie—*Kung Fu Panda*—released in 2008 deals with the 'Dragon Scroll', which is said to hold the secret to limitless power. When Po, the lovable Panda, opens the scroll, it reveals nothing but a blank. There may be a number of so-called trade secrets which may not be secrets at all. It may include one of the best kept trade secrets—the Coke formula. Who knows? But, till the time the world believes it to be a secret, it remains a secret. A lot of effort has to be put in, to keep secret things 'secret'. Once it is known to public, it does not remain a secret. The process is irreversible.

In business, it is important to anticipate what one's competitor is planning to do. In fact, knowledge about competitor's trade secrets is of utmost importance. Knowing such details facilitates formulation of the right business strategy. Comprehension and understanding of the competitor's secrets can help in gaining a competitive edge over him, by launching counter measures and strategies to outdo him. Thus, it is advisable to get maximum insight into the competitor's business, without letting him know of one's own. The Coca-Cola formula is a well kept secret. Even some of the roadside tea stall owners have a secret ingredient for making their tea 'different' from others. Super chefs may have their own secret way of crushing a mint leaf in the palm to get that special flavour. It has been well depicted in the movie *Thank You for Smoking* by Captain to Nick Naylor. Some of the bartenders might be following James Bond's secret of making a fine drink—shaken, not stirred. Can these be called trade secrets?

THE LAW

The Roman law created a cause of action called 'actio servi corrupti' (an action for corrupting a slave), which was used to punish unscrupulous businessmen who would 'corrupt' slaves by bribery or intimidation into disclosing their owner's confidential business information. European countries developed trade protection law and later the English and American courts recognized it. Japan came up with such a law very late, due to a different culture. Socially, it was not considered acceptable to insist on formal confidentiality agreements while in business, being wedded to one's job for a lifetime reduced the risk of trade secrets being made public.

Article 39 of the Trade-Related Aspects of Intellectual Property Rights (TRIPs) provides for protection of trade secrets by member nations. These nations are under an obligation to protect undisclosed information and data, submitted to governments or governmental agencies. The nations must enact and enforce laws so that natural and legal persons (companies, etc.), have an opportunity to prevent disclosure of information lawfully within their control. It applies to confidential information and trade secrets which have commercial value—as these are secret—and reasonable steps have been taken by the owner to keep them secret.

In the United States, trade secrets are protected by state laws. Since 1979, most of the states follow the model law—The Uniform Trade Secrets Act—in one form or another. The law interprets 'trade secret' in the most liberal manner and includes information related to a formula, pattern, compilation, program, device, method, technique, or process. Such information derives 'independent economic value'—actual or potential—from not being generally known to—and is the subject of 'reasonable efforts' to maintain its secrecy.

There is no similar law in India and confidential information and trade secrets are protected primarily with the help of contracts. In the absence of any explicit contract, protection is provided on equitable grounds.

SALIENT FEATURES

Unlike other branches of intellectual property—for instance patents are for twenty years, copyright for sixty years after the death of the author, etc.—there is no term of protection for a trade secret. It can be kept a secret till the time it becomes public knowledge. The moment it is disclosed, the protection is lost. However, if a person finds the trade secret or confidential information by independent discovery or reverse engineering, that person is not liable for prosecution. The cost of keeping a 'trade secret' secret and 'confidential information' confidential may be, at times, quite high—besides the cost of keeping it secret, the litigation cost in cases of breach may be prohibitive. Many a time, it may dissuade a company from keeping things confidential. It is a decision which the company needs to make keeping in mind the commercial value of trade secret and the security expense and risks involved. Licensing of a 'trade secret' or 'commercial information' is a thorny exercise. By its innate nature, the owner (licensor) wants a price for something confidential and secret and therefore doesn't want to let the prospective buyer know the details. The buyer (licensee) wishes to know what it is so that he can make up his mind. It is very difficult to have the meeting of minds and arrive at a mutual consensus on the way forward.

THREE ESSENTIAL ELEMENTS

(1) The subject matter must be a secret capable of adding economic value. The purpose is to ensure that no one claims protection for something which is known in a particular trade.

(2) The owner must take reasonable precautions to keep it a secret. The purpose is to ensure that no one claims protection for something which was flowing freely to competitors at one time and later the owner claims that the competitors got the information in a wrongful manner.

(3) In cases of breach, the owner must prove that the competitor got the information in a wrongful manner.

Any information imparted in confidence is 'confidential information'. Any such information related to trade, industry or business is termed 'trade secret'. When we say 'any' information, it does not as a matter of fact mean 'any' because such an information must be 'confidential' and a 'secret'. It has to be tested on the anvil of reasonableness. The simple understanding is that such information should not be in public domain, it should not be obvious and there must be something 'secretive' about it. For instance, if A tells B in confidence that the Sun rises in the east, by any stretch of imagination it does not become 'confidential information'. If A tells B in confidence a trade secret—the formula for making a successful movie—two brothers with similar tattoos on their backs separated in the village fair in childhood and meet later in life, one as a robber and the other as a police inspector, it does not become a 'trade secret' as it is well known and has been used by a number of film producers.

Thus it is important that the information is not known to the public at large. It must not be obvious. It must be disclosed only to a very few select people by the owner of the information.

Owner Believes the Information to be Confidential

One prerequisite is that the owner must believe that the information is confidential and a secret. It is not necessary that no one else knows about it. There may be persons who know about it either by permission of the owner or through their own efforts or by serendipity. But, till the time such information is not in public domain, it remains 'confidential information' or 'trade secret'. The problem the owner shall face in such a scenario is how to keep such a person silent. It will depend on how much such information can be commercially exploited. For instance, if A comes to know of B's business plan, which is confidential and known only to B's team members (B1, B2, B3...Bn), A may blackmail B. If B thinks that it does not affect him even if A discloses it to the world, there is no problem for B. However, if B thinks otherwise and wishes to keep A silent, B can enter into a contract with A for this purpose. In case B does not know that A knows B's plan, B will continue to believe that the information has not been leaked to anyone and it is safe to continue with the business plan. Such a state of affairs is most undesirable on the part of B, as it shows that B has been living in a fool's paradise and has not taken adequate measures to protect the confidential information. The law, however, provides protection even in such cases when the owner believes that the information has been confidential and a secret. It should be a reasonable belief. In case B goes on to tell such information indiscreetly to every one he meets as if discussing the day's weather, even if he starts the conversation with, 'this is between you and me...', there is no protection given by law as his understanding of keeping the information a secret is not reasonable.

REASONABLE PRECAUTIONS

The owner must take 'reasonable' precaution to keep such information a secret. What such precautionary steps are depends on the information and the context. If it is highly confidential, all foreseeable precautions must be taken. The 'will' of a multi-billionaire, Coca-Cola formula, Tata's Rs 1-lakh car (before its launch and christening as Nano), etc. all fall in this category. In such a scenario abundant precaution is to be practiced. It may not be adequate protection even if it is kept inside a two-foot steel locker, if the key is not well-protected. Reasonable measures must be taken to protect the key. After taking all such precautions, if the owner keeps on talking about it in the elevator, taxi or cafeteria, it defeats the purpose. Reasonableness shall be judged by the holistic behaviour of the owner. It is reported that Tata Motors had taken unprecedented security measures to keep Nano a secret prior to its unveiling at the 9th Auto Expo at Pragati Maidan in New Delhi on January 10, 2008. There was not even a whiff of Nano to the paparazzi. At this point one distinction needs to be made—the efforts have to be 'reasonable' and law does not expect the owner to make efforts, which may be made by a paranoid, who is obsessed with something and distrusts everyone.

The American Express Case

Priya Puri was working as head of wealth management, Northern Region at the New Delhi office of American Express—AmEx, the international credit card major. She had joined AmEx in March 2001, in the credit cards division and was transferred to the wealth management division in 2003 and was made the head of that division in April 2005. AmEx had named and styled various business activities of wealth management as 'iWealth View', which had products like demand products, term deposits, and mutual funds. As head of the Northern India wealth management division, Priya had a team of thirteen financial concierges and three regional managers. She had access to highly confidential information and trade secrets of AmEx such as customer data and information. According to AmEx, it had taken all reasonable steps to ensure the protection of confidential information with individual password and authorization to only such persons who could access that information.

Priya submitted her resignation letter in September 2005 with a thirty-day notice. At this time, AmEx came to know that she had got an exhaustive list of large number of customers and their investment accounts prepared. According to AmEx, she had used her official position to get the entire customer data which was confidential and to which she had no access. AmEx also came to know that she had planned to join a competitor and was persuading customers to shift their accounts from AmEx to the competitor.

Talks between AmEx and Priya to resolve this dispute failed and in October 2005, AmEx terminated Priya's services primarily on the ground that she had disclosed confidential information to persons which was not in connection with AmEx's business. The other grounds were compromising the position of trust held by her as an employee, failing to avoid any conflict of interest between her personal interest and that of AmEx, using confidential information and trade secrets for her own benefit, violating AmEx's customer privacy policy, failing to return customer list and details, using them for personal benefit or for any of AmEx's competitor and violating AmEx's intellectual property rights.

Regarding confidential information, relevant clauses of the terms and conditions of her employment contract stated:

> You will maintain the confidentiality of all the information that you will be exposed to and will not divulge any information pertaining to the operations of the Company or any of its affiliates to any one without the express written permission of your superior.
>
> You will not, at any time, while in employment with the Company, use other than in reference to the business of the Company and in the course of your duties any such confidential information OR after cessation of employment with the Company, use to disclose to anyone else such confidential information and you will also undertake to indemnify the Company and its affiliates from any loss or damage arising from any breach of this undertaking.

Besides the contractual clauses, AmEx enforced a 'code of conduct' which was applicable to all the employees. Priya had attended various training sessions on code of conduct. This code of conduct provides in great detail almost everything conceivable as intellectual property, including confidential information and trade secrets. It is pretty long but I feel it's worth going through. So, the part related to intellectual property, confidential information and trade secrets is reproduced verbatim:

CODE OF CONDUCT

Intellectual Property

You must protect and, when appropriate, enforce the Company's intellectual property rights.

The company's intellectual property is among its most valuable assets. Intellectual property refers to creations of the human mind that are protected by various national laws and international treaties, in a fashion similar to real property (i.e, land). Intellectual property includes copyrights, patents, trademarks, trade secrets, design rights, logos, know-how and other intangible industrial or commercial property.

Confidential Information and Trade Secrets

You must protect confidential information and trade secrets, and prevent such information from being improperly disclosed to others inside or outside the Company.

During the course of your employment, you may learn confidential information about the Company that is not known to the general public or to competitors. Information of this sort is considered a trade secret if it provides the Company with a competitive or economic advantage over its competitors. Confidential information or trade secrets may not be disclosed outside the Company or used for your own or someone else's benefit. These obligations apply both during, and subsequent to, your employment with American Express. When you leave the Company, you must return any and all copies of materials containing the Company's confidential information or trade secrets in your possession.

Some examples of American Express' confidential information or trade secrets include:-

Customer lists; the terms, discount rates or fees offered to particular customers; marketing or strategic plans; and software, risk models, tools and other system developments. Within the Company, confidential information and trade secrets may be divulged only to other employees who need the information to carry out their duties. When discussing confidential information or trade secrets, you must not do so in places where you can be overheard, such as taxis, elevators, the Company cafeteria or restaurants. In addition, you should not communicate or transmit confidential information or trade secrets by non-secure methods (e.g. cell phones, non-secure email, hotel faxes, etc.).

Trademarks, Copyrights and Patents

You must protect the Company's trademarks, copyrights and patents. Publications, documentation, training materials, computer codes, and other works of authorship you develop for the Company are the types of material that can be protected by copyrights. You may also create, discover or develop software, methods, systems or other patentable inventions when performing your responsibilities or utilizing information or resources available to you in connection with your employment. To the extent permitted by law, as an employee or a contractor, you agree that all such works of authorship and inventions, whether or not patentable or protectable by copyright, trade secret or trademark, are assigned to the Company whether they be improvements, derivatives, designs, technologies, written materials, programs or any other works. Our logos and the name 'American Express' are examples of Company trademarks recognized around the world. You must use Company trademarks properly and consistently, and must protect the Company's goodwill and brand investments from being used by others for their own advantage. You also must advise senior management or the General Counsel's Office if you become aware that others are improperly using the

Company's trademarks. Certain jurisdictions have their own laws that may supersede elements of this policy. In those cases, the laws of that jurisdiction prevail. If you think an invention may be eligible for a patent or are unsure about a proposed use of Company trademarks, copyrights or patents, you should consult the General Counsel's Office.

The termination letter included a request to Priya to return AmEx's confidential information and data (list of customers with account details) and to refrain from soliciting any of its customers. Priya had returned the laptop, car, corporate card, identity card, mobile phone, and denied having possession of any confidential material of AmEx.

Thereafter, AmEx filed a suit in the Delhi High Court for perpetual injunction against Priya seeking primarily restrain against her from using any confidential information or trying to solicit AmEx's customers and directing her to deliver all confidential information in general and the customers' list with account details in particular. Priya contested the claims of AmEx largely on two grounds, that she did not get any list prepared and that the said information—names, addresses, etc. of the customers—was not confidential.

The Delhi High Court discussed the matter at great length and decided that first, Priya had no reason to get such a list prepared as she already knew it and secondly, such information cannot be categorized as 'confidential information'. Priya knew very well the names, addresses, and financial details of the high income clients. As a matter of fact, she approached a number of them to do business with the bank. They themselves were willing to disclose such details to her. In such a scenario can she be restrained from taking those details because such details have already been given by the clients to AmEx? Therefore, it cannot be inferred that Priya did not have the information which is touted as confidential and sacrosanct. Moreover, Priya could not be restrained from soliciting AmEx's customers as it would create a situation of 'once a customer of American Express, always a customer of American Express'. It is the prerogative of a person to bank with any banking company. Priya could not even be restrained from using the said information while working with the next employer as the Court felt that she could not be directed not to use her work experience.

SPRING BOARD DOCTRINE

The idea of confidential information has been in existence since ages. However, there has been a certain degree of confusion about it. British courts have decided in a catena of judgments that a person who had obtained information in confidence should not be allowed to use it as a spring-board for activities detrimental to the person who made the confidential communication. This applies to all such information which can be ascertained by actual inspection by any member of the public.

Now, this does not make sense in extreme cases. For instance, if A tells B in confidence that New Delhi is the capital of India, is B restrained from using such information as it is confidential? Of course, not! On the other extreme, if A tells B in confidence that the secret formula for making gold is 'x+y = gold', B is surely restrained from using this information as it is confidential and B should not use this information as a spring-board for making his own gold and selling it to the detriment of A. Thus, it depends on the context.

In the AmEx case, the information was not held to be confidential and Priya was allowed to use it even after leaving

AmEx. The spring-board doctrine was not followed. The court held that the so-called confidential information was capable of ascertainment by an independent canvass at a small expense and in a very limited period of time. This is a bit surprising because the spring-board doctrine says that it applies to *all such information which can be ascertained by actual inspection by any member of the public*. But, AmEx lost the case principally for the reason that it did not go to the court with 'clean hands'. It did not provide all the details to the court and also did not give a very convincing reason as to why Priya asked another person to prepare the list of customers when she could have done it herself. She was not computer illiterate, so what was the need for her to ask anyone else to provide a printout of customers' list? She could have done the same after knowing the password. And, if she was the North India head, why did she not have access to the customers' list? It all seemed unconvincing.

The court rightly held that it was all an afterthought by AmEx to pressurise Priya either not to leave the bank or to teach her a lesson and curtail her future prospect for employment. AmEx tried to use the garb of confidentiality clause in the employment contract and failed.

The Diljeet Titus Case

This is a very interesting case of a famous Delhi lawyer, Diljeet Titus—equally famous for his collection of cars—who started his law firm, Titus & Co., in 1997 and according to him 'retained' a number of lawyers as associates. Four of them, Seema Ahluwalia Jhingan, Alishan Naqvee, Dimpy Mohanty, and Alfred A. Adebare, parted ways sometime in 2003–4. They set up their own law firm. Interestingly, Alfred was from Nigeria and did not have a licence to practice law in India. According to Diljeet, before leaving his firm, Alfred went to the office of the law firm after office hours with a CD-Writer and copied all the confidential information from the Local Area Network (LAN). Then, he sent email attachments of other confidential material to his three partners and himself, stole licensed CDs of all foreign judgments, precedents, etc. and over 3000 visiting cards given by different clients. Diljeet asked the four of them to refrain from using that material, data, and information but they refused. Diljeet claimed that they were his full-time employees and worked on his directions, whereas they claimed that they were partners in the partnership firm and as they had prepared most of these documents, they had a right to use them. The noted politician-lawyer, Arun Jaitley appeared for Diljeet and argued that though there was no explicit contract between Diljeet and the four lawyers, yet there was an implicit term of confidentiality between them, which they had breached.

The Court held that there was a contract of service and the four lawyers were working on the directions of Diljeet. No doubt there was a copyright in the material created, but that belonged to the employer, Diljeet. The other four lawyers had breached the confidence and trust, which clients had reposed in Diljeet and were restrained from using the copied and 'stolen' material.

This is a landmark judgment and one of its kinds. A dispute among lawyers is not uncommon, but taking it to the court and fighting a long legal battle is surely uncommon. A comparison with the American Express case highlights that the mere presence of a contract—brief or detailed—is no guarantee for protection of one's confidential information and trade secrets. AmEx had a detailed contract, yet failed to get the desired relief from the court. One valuable conclusion is that—'one needs to go to the court with clean hands'. AmEx messed up its case by including unconvincing stories and the four lawyers in the Titus case literally copied and stole the material. Had the four lawyers gone to Diljeet and told him that as the work belonged to them, they would like to have a copy, things would have been very different. Similarly, had AmEx told the real reason for filing the case against Priya and also used the right legal tools to achieve that purpose, it might have borne a different result. But, we need to remember that these laws have been made to keep the offender in control. Luckily, the courts in India interpret laws with the changing aspirations of people.

FOOD FOR THOUGHT

In August 2008, Thomas Weisel Partners LLC, a US based investment banking outfit, sued French banking giant BNP Paribas and Mr Chakravarty, one of its Indian employee, alleging data theft from its Indian subsidiary. Thomas Wiesel wanted a California court to hear the case and claimed that the Indian legal system was weak in protecting intellectual property. What do you think happened?

FILL IN THE BLANKS

i)   Actio servi _____.

ii)   _____ precautions have to be taken to protect confidential information.

iii)   To get protection from law, the owner of any such information must believe that the information is _____.

TRUE OR FALSE

a)   Contracts guarantee protection of confidential information.

b)   'Most of the politicians are corrupt' is a good example of confidential information.

c)   Corporate espionage is a healthy competitive practice.

d)   All over the world, the law regarding trade secrets is uniform.

KEY TO FILL IN THE BLANKS

i)   Corrupti

ii) Reasonable

iii) Confidential

TRUE FALSE

a) False

b) False

c) False

d) False

8

Epilogue

Philosophically, protection of intellectual property may be for either economic or moral reasons. The idea of morality and its intersection with law have long been the subject of debate. Whether every law is moral or every aspect of morality has been enacted into law, it is difficult to say with surety. The basic idea of ownership—whether tangible property or intangible, intellectual property—is related to the legal environment of a particular place which may allow ownership of all properties including intellectual property, or it may allow ownership of only some of these properties. Even if ownership is allowed by law, it will have no meaning if there is no proper protection of the right to own it. Enforcement machinery has to be created which includes 'instruments' such as different Acts passed by the parliament, 'institutions' like courts, IP tribunals, appellate bodies, functional intellectual property offices and above all, 'individuals' who can make all this work.

It is quite heartening that in the last two decades a number of efforts have been made to have these 3 Is—instruments, institutions, and individuals—in place. A lot more still needs to be done. As the legal environment has an impact on business, similarly businesses also have an impact on the legal environment. It has become quite difficult to find sufficient numbers of qualified persons to man the positions which have been created in different IP institutions—administrative, scientific, quasi-judicial, etc. It has become a regular practice that new incumbents, after spending a couple of years with these public institutions, are lured by private companies and many times it is difficult for these public institutions to stop them from joining private companies. This is clearly proving to be 'private gains, public losses'. In such a scenario it is very difficult to expand the working of these institutions because there is a constant shortage of the right kind of people to join public institutions.

Another issue of serious concern is the gap between technology and law. As technology develops very fast—particularly in computers, Internet, biotechnology, etc.—there is a need to keep pace with it by enacting the required laws and anticipating the needs of the future. Most of the time law follows technology. In such a situation the courts are left with no choice but to use the existing law, extrapolate it, and try their best to decide the dispute in hand keeping in mind the changing aspirations of the people. An illustration can be the use of the Indian Telegraph Act, 1885 for resolving a dispute about an MMS sent by a school student in Delhi about four years ago.

The global legal environment is directly affected by the political and economic situation in different countries, particularly in the US. Of late, protectionist tendencies are quite high in the US, creating a lot of problems for the expansion of global trade and services and it may possibly have a negative impact on global treaties regarding intellectual property rights. The business of most multinational companies is based on protection of their patents, trademarks, copyrights, designs, and trade secrets in all the countries where they do business. In the absence of mutual recognition it will become difficult for American companies and other companies from the developed world to receive the desired level of protection in India and China—often blamed for noticeable piracy—and thus their business interests are going to suffer. It may not be surprising that India and China and other developing countries harden their stand and do not allow the high level of protection to foreign trademarks, foreign patents, and copyrights registered abroad.

We hope that such clouds of over-zealous protectionism will soon go away and the whole world will again move in the direction of uniform, harmonious, and efficacious intellectual property rights laws—the primary goal of the TRIPS Agreement.

Appendix

IMPORTANT DEFINITIONS

(A) The Patents Act, 1970

Patent – Section 2 (1) (m) – patent means a patent for any invention granted under this Act.

Invention – Section 2 (1) (j) – invention means a new product or process involving an inventive step and capable of industrial application.

Inventive Step – Section 2 (1) (ja) – inventive step means a feature of an invention that involves technical advance as compared to the existing knowledge or having economic significance or both and that makes the invention not obvious to a person skilled in the art.

New Invention – Section 2 (1) (l) – new invention means any invention or technology which has not been anticipated by publication in any document or used in the country or elsewhere in the world before the date of filing of patent application with complete specification, i.e. the subject matter has not fallen in public domain or that it does not form part of the state of the art.

(B) The Copyright Act, 1957

Meaning of Copyright – Section 14–copyright means the exclusive right subject to the provisions of this Act, to do or authorise the doing of any of the following acts in respect of a work or any substantial part thereof, namely:

(a)   in the case of a *literary, dramatic or musical work*, not being a computer programme,—

   (i)   to reproduce the work in any material form including the storing of it in any medium by electronic means;
   (ii)   to issue copies of the work to the public not being copies already in circulation;
   (iii)   to perform the work in public, or communicate it to the public;
   (iv)   to make any cinematograph film or sound recording in respect of the work;
   (v)   to make any translation of the work;
   (vi)   to make any adaptation of the work;
   (vii) to do, in relation to a translation or an adaptation of the work, any of the acts specified in relation to the work in sub-clauses (i) to (vi);

(b)   in the case of a *computer programme*,—

   (i)   to do any of the acts specified in clause (a);
   (ii)   to sell or give on commercial rental or offer for sale or for commercial rental any copy of the computer programme:

Provided that such commercial rental does not apply in respect of computer programmes where the programme itself is not the essential object of the rental.

(c)   in the case of an *artistic work*,—

  (i)   to reproduce the work in any material form including depiction in three dimensions of a two dimensional work or in two dimensions of a three dimensional work;
  (ii)   to communicate the work to the public;
  (iii) to issue copies of the work to the public not being copies already in circulation;
  (iv)   to include the work in any cinematograph film;
  (v)   to make any adaptation of the work;
  (vi)   to do in relation to an adaptation of the work any of the acts specified in relation to the work in sub-clauses (i) to (iv);

(d)   in the case of a *cinematograph film*,—

  (i)   to make a copy of the film including a photograph of any image forming part thereof;
  (ii)   to sell or give on hire or offer for sale or hire, any copy of the film, regardless of whether such copy has been sold or given on hire on earlier occasions;
  (iii) to communicate the film to the public;

(e)   in the case of a *sound recording*,—

  (i)   to make any other sound recording embodying it;
  (ii)   to sell or give on hire, or offer for sale or hire, any copy of the sound recording, regardless of whether such copy has been sold or given on hire on earlier occasions;
  (iii) to communicate the sound recording to the public.

Explanation—For the purposes of this section, a copy which has been sold once shall be deemed to be a copy already in circulation.

Artistic Work – Section 2 (c) - artistic work means,—

(i)   a painting, a sculpture, a drawing (including a diagram, map, chart or plan), an engraving or a photograph, whether or not any such work possesses artistic quality;

(ii)   a work of architecture; and

(iii) any other work of artistic craftsmanship;

Author – Section 2 (d) - author means,—

(i)   in relation to a literary or dramatic work, the author of the work;

(ii)   in relation to a musical work, the composer;

(iii) in relation to an artistic work other than a photograph, the artist;

(iv)   in relation to a photograph, the person taking the photograph;

(v)   in relation to a cinematograph film or sound recording, the producer; and

(vi)   in relation to any literary, dramatic, musical or artistic work which is computer-generated, the person who causes the work to be created

Cinematograph Film – Section 2 (f) - cinematograph film means any work of visual recording on any medium produced through a process from which a moving image may be produced by any means and includes a sound recording accompanying such visual recording and "cinematograph" shall be construed as including any work produced by any process analogous to cinematography including video films.

Composer – Section 2 (ffa) – composer, in relation to a musical work, means the person who composes the music regardless of whether he records it in any form of graphical notation.

Dramatic Work – Section 2 (h) – dramatic work includes any piece of recitation, choreographic work or entertainment in dumb show, the scenic arrangement or acting, form of which is fixed in writing or otherwise but does not include a cinematograph film.

Engravings – Section 2 (i) – engravings include etchings, lithographs, wood-cuts, prints and other similar works, not being photographs.

Lecture – Section 2 (n) – lecture includes address, speech and sermon.

Literary Work – Section 2 (o) – literary work includes computer programmes, tables and compilations including computer databases.

Musical Work – Section 2 (p) – musical work means a work consisting of music and includes any graphical notation of such work but does not include any words or any action intended to be sung, spoken or performed with the music.

Performance – Section 2 (q) – performance, in relation to performer's right, means any visual or acoustic presentation made live by one or more performers.

Performer – Section 2 (qq) – performer includes an actor, singer, musician, dancer, acrobat, juggler, conjurer, snake charmer, a person delivering a lecture or any other person who makes a performance.

Producer – Section 2 (uu) – producer, in relation to a cinematograph film or sound recording, means a person who takes the initiative and responsibility for making the work.

Sound Recording – Section 2 (xx) – sound recording means a recording of sounds from which such sounds may be produced regardless of the medium on which such recording is made or the method by which the sounds are produced.

Work – Section 2 (y) – work means any of the following works, namely:—

(i)   a literary, dramatic, musical or artistic work;

(ii)   a cinematograph film;

(iii)   a sound recording.

(C) The Trademarks Act, 1999

Mark – Section 2 (1) (m) – "mark" includes a device, brand, heading, label, ticket, name, signature, word, letter, numeral, shape of goods, packaging or combination of colours or any combination thereof.

Trade Mark – Section 2 (1) (zb) - "trade mark" means a mark capable of being represented graphically and which is capable of distinguishing the goods or services of one person from those of others and may include shape of goods, their packaging and combination of colours , and

(i)   in relation to Chapter XII (other than section 107), a registered trade mark or mark used in relation to goods or services for the purpose of indicating or so as to indicate a connection in the course of trade between the goods or services, as the case may be, and some person having the right as proprietor to use the mark, and

(ii)   in relation to other provisions of this Act, a mark used or proposed to be used in relation to goods or services for the purpose of indicating or so to indicate to a connection in the course of trade between the goods or services, as the case may be, and some person having the right, either as proprietor or by way of permitted user, to use the mark whether with or without any indication of the identity of that person, and includes a certification trade mark or collective mark.

Well-known Trade Mark – Section 2 (1) (zg) "well-known trade mark" in relation to any goods or services, means a mark which has become so to the substantial segment of the public which uses such goods or receives such services that the use of such mark in relation to other goods or services would be likely to be taken as indicating a connection in the course of trade or rendering of services between those goods or services and a person using the mark in relation to the first mentioned goods or services.

Certification Trade Mark – Section 2 (1) (e) – "certification trade mark" means a mark capable of distinguishing the goods or services in connection with which it is used in the course of trade which are certified by the proprietor of the mark in respect of origin, material, mode of manufacture of goods or performance of services, quality, accuracy or other characteristics from goods or services not so certified and registrable as such under Chapter IX in respect of those goods or services in the name, as proprietor of the certification trade mark, of that person.

Collective Mark – Section 2 (1) (g) – "collective mark" means a trade mark distinguishing the goods or services of members of an association of persons (not being a partnership within the meaning of the Indian Partnership Act, 1932) which is the proprietor of the mark from those of others.

Deceptively Similar – Section 2 (1) (h) – A mark shall be deemed to be deceptively similar to another mark if it so nearly resembles that other mark as to be likely to deceive or cause confusion;

Package – Section 2 (1) (q) – "package" includes any case, box, container, covering, folder, receptacle, vessel, casket, bottle, wrapper, label, band, ticket, reel, frame, capsule, cap, lid, stopper and cork.

Service – Section 2 (1) (z) – "service" means service of any description which is made available to potential users and includes the provisions of services in connection with business of any industrial or commercial matters such as banking, communication, education, financing, insurance, chit funds, real estate, transport, storage, material treatment, processing, supply of electrical or other energy, boarding, lodging, entertainment, amusement, construction, repair, conveying of news or information and advertising.

(D) The Designs Act, 2000

Design – Section 2 (d) – "design" means only the features of shape, configuration, pattern, ornament or composition of lines or colours applied to any article whether in two dimensional or three dimensional or in both forms, by any industrial process or means, whether manual mechanical or chemical, separate or combined, which in the finished article appeal to and are judged solely by the eye; but does not include any mode or principle of construction or anything which is in substance a mere mechanical device, and does not include any trade mark as defined in clause (v) of sub-section (1) of section 2 of the Trade and Merchandise Marks Act, 1958 or property mark as defined in section 479 of the Indian Penal Code or any artistic work as defined in clause (c) of section 2 of the Copyright Act, 1957.

Trade Mark – The Trade and Merchandise Mark Act, 1958 – Section 2 (1) (v) - "trade mark" means -

(i) in relation to Chapter X (other than section 81), a registered trade mark or a mark used in relation to goods for the purpose of indicating or so as to indicate a connection in the course of trade between the goods and some person having the right as proprietor to use the mark; and

(ii) in relation to the other provisions of this Act, a mark used or proposed to be used in relation to goods for the purpose of indicating or so as to indicate a connection in course of trade between the goods and some person having the right, either as proprietor or as registered user, to use the mark whether with or without any indication of the identity of that person, and includes a certification trade mark registered as such under the provisions of Chapter VIII.

Property Mark – The Indian Penal Code – Section 479 – Property mark - A mark used for denoting that movable property belongs to a particular person is called a property mark.

Original – Section 2 (g) – "original", in relation to a design, means originating from the author of such design and includes the cases which though old in themselves yet are new in their application.

(E) The Geographical Indications of Goods (Registration and Protection) Act, 1999

Indication – Section 2 (1) (g) – "indication" includes any name, geographical or figurative representation or any combination of them conveying or suggesting the geographical origin of goods to which it applies.

Geographical Indication – Section 2 (1) (e) – "geographical indication", in relation to goods, means an indication which identifies such goods as agricultural goods, natural goods or manufactured goods as originating, or manufactured in the territory of country, or a region or locality in that territory, where a given quality, reputation or other characteristic of such goods is essentially attributable to its geographical origin and in case where such goods are manufactured goods one of the activities of either the production or of processing or preparation of the goods concerned takes place in such territory, region or locality, as the case may be.

Explanation – For the purposes of this clause, any name which is not the name of country, region or locality of that country shall also be considered as the geographical indication if it relates to a specific geographical area and is used upon or in relation to particular goods originating from that country, region or locality, as the case may be.

Goods – Section 2 (1) (f) – "goods" means any agricultural, natural or manufactured goods or any goods of handicraft or of industry and includes food stuff.

Registered Proprietor – Section 2 (1) (n) – "registered proprietor", in relation to a geographical indication, means any association of persons or of producer or any organisation for the time being entered in the register as proprietor of the geographical indication.

A note on IIMA Business Books

The IIM Ahmedabad Business Books bring key issues in management and business to a general audience. With a wealth of information and illustrations from contemporary Indian businesses, these non-academic and user-friendly books from the faculty of IIM Ahmedabad are essential corporate reading. www.iimabooks.com

Would you like to participate

in the IIMA Guru Yatra?

For more details visit

www.iimabooks.com

OTHER BOOKS IN THIS SERIES

INDIA'S BESTSELLING BUSINESS BOOKS SERIES

IIM
AHMEDABAD
BUSINESS BOOKS

**STRATEGIES FOR
THE FUTURE**
Understanding International Business

AJEET N. MATHUR

INDIA'S BESTSELLING BUSINESS BOOKS SERIES

IIM
AHMEDABAD
BUSINESS BOOKS

**BUSINESS LAW
FOR MANAGERS**
Kaleidoscopic Tales

ANURAG K. AGARWAL

INDIA'S BESTSELLING BUSINESS BOOKS SERIES

IIM
AHMEDABAD
BUSINESS BOOKS

**DAY TO DAY
ECONOMICS**

SATISH Y. DEODHAR

INDIA'S BESTSELLING BUSINESS BOOKS SERIES

IIM
AHMEDABAD
BUSINESS BOOKS

**CONTRACT
TERMS ARE
COMMON SENSE**

AKHILESHWAR PATHAK